THE
PRODUCTIVITY
FACTOR

THE
PRODUCTIVITY
FACTOR

How to Accomplish Twice as Much in Half the Time

DR. JOHN DEMARTINI

Published 2023 by Gildan Media LLC
aka G&D Media
www.GandDmedia.com

Front cover design by David Rheinhardt of Pyrographx

Interior design by Meghan Day Healey of Story Horse, LLC.

Library of Congress Cataloging-in-Publication Data is available
upon request

ISBN: 978-1-7225-0629-2

10   9   8   7   6   5   4   3   2   1

Contents

Preface

Are you maximizing your daily productivity, or are you not? Are you even in a position to tell? How are you defining and measuring your productivity?

Here's how the US Bureau of Labor Statistics defines it: "Productivity is a measure of economic performance that compares the amount of goods and services produced (*output*) with the amount of *inputs* used to produce those goods and services."

To put it simply: more output with less input.

Why is this important?

Your fulfillment in life will be partly proportionate to your productivity—the quality and quantity of your work or service. For the rest of your life, you will spend most of your waking hours doing some kind of work, or service. Although it may take on many forms during different phases of your evolution, work will remain a principal fact of your life. You will be solving problems, answering questions, tackling challenges, overcoming obstacles, filling needs, organizing chaos, or simply moving objects for yourself and others. Even those who imagine that they are too young or have retired are still doing some form of work or service.

Your work can be productive or unproductive, fulfilling or unfulfilling, inspiring or uninspiring. It is up to you. You can do what you love and love what you do—or not. Inspiring and meaningful work will energize you and make you feel youthful or even ageless. Uninspiring work will drain you and make you feel prematurely old. As a billionaire once said, "Find out how to do the work you love to do and you will seldom, if ever, perceive your work as work ever again." You will love to work. Even "hard" work will feel as if you are hardly working.

Your work can be one of your greatest satisfactions and allies in life, or it can become one of your most frustrating enemies. When you use your time wisely and productively and make every day count by doing work that genuinely inspires you, you will have more energy at the end of the day than when you started.

Your time is your most precious resource, and everyone has exactly the same amount of it. You have 60 seconds a minute, 60 minutes per hour, 24 hours per day, 168 hours per week, 52 weeks per year. How are you filling your time? "Wasting" your time could be viewed as "wasting" your life.

How many more years do you intend to live? What working actions of meaningful service do you intend to fill your remaining time with? Are you making the most of the remaining minutes, hours, days, weeks, months, and years of this brief and mortal life? Are you masterfully planning your life, taking command and becoming captain of your ship and a prophet of your own inspired destiny? Are you willing to transcend immediate gratification in favor of your long-term vision of service and reward—regardless of your chronological age?

Any aspect of your work that you choose not to direct and govern will govern you. You can become a slave to unfulfilling work, or you can become your work's master and provide heartfelt service.

Wisely working means achieving your primary tasks at hand, fulfilling your chief aim over time, and continually producing meaningful and advantageous results. You can work less and accomplish more by working according to your highest priorities, or you can work more and accomplish less by working according to lower priorities.

When you know what is truly valuable to you—your true higher values or priorities—and you set sail toward your highest value-driven chief aim, or purpose, you awaken your natural love for working, solving problems, and serving. You activate your inner leader, and you spontaneously become inspired from within to fulfill your higher, most meaningful values. You'll be eager to get up and do what is most important and authentic to you, and the world won't be able to wait to get your service.

The true key to maximizing your productivity is knowing and congruently and consistently fulfilling your highest value or chief aim in life. When you have clear, purposeful intentions and live in alignment with your highest values, you automatically begin to walk your talk and awaken your natural inborn leader. You expand your space and time horizons to fulfill your working dreams, and you live longer. You can then focus on planting flowers in the garden of your working mind instead of pulling weeds.

In this book, I'll give you proven, clear, and certain keys to productivity. You'll learn:

- How to identify your highest value in life.
- How to link the work you are doing now to that value.
- How to make your vocation your vacation.
- How to live through intrinsic inspiration rather than mere extrinsic motivation.
- How to fulfill your *telos*, or your principal goal or objective in life.
- How to prioritize your daily actions.
- How to appreciate the natural balance between support and challenge in the path of fulfilling your greatest achievement.
- The law of sustainable fair exchange and the way to use it to fulfill your purpose.
- How to transcend or transform distractions.
- The power of a clear and authentic mission statement coming from the heart.
- The power of saying no to low priority distractions.
- The true nature of self-governance and mastery.

And much, much more. As a bonus, I've included an appendix with some principles and methods on how to maximize one of the greatest productivity tools of all—reading.

Use the principles and methodologies in this book to determine your highest values and achieve greater productivity, meaning, and fulfillment. Now it is time to wisely get to work. You still have a great life ahead and a vast world of loved ones to serve.

Chapter 1

The Power of Values

The key to productivity is simple: it is living congruently and acting in accord with your own true highest values.

Every human being lives with a set of priorities, a set of values. This set of values is unique to each individual.

Whatever is highest or most important on this unique list of values is what you are most likely to be spontaneously inspired from within to do or fulfill. You are much less likely to require any extrinsic motivation, such as the promise of reward or fear of punishment, to get it done.

In my case, my highest values are teaching, researching, and writing. I love these activities, so no one has to externally motivate me to do them. When it comes to driving or cooking, which are lower on my values, I have little inclination to do them and will instead outsource or delegate them.

It's the same in your life. You will have actions that you are spontaneously inspired to do. You won't procrastinate in doing them; instead, you'll make time for them. They reflect your highest values.

Some individuals find it difficult to identify their highest values because they think they "should" be different from what they truly are.

You may be trying to live in someone else's values. For example, you may perceive that you "should" have family as your highest value instead of work. Or perhaps you think you "should" have spirituality as your highest value instead of physical well-being.

This situation may have come about because some people have been telling you what your highest values and priorities "should" be. You may be allowing their voices to cloud the clarity of your own true and current value hierarchy. If this is the case, you may not be consciously honoring your own true highest values. You may not be consciously living and acting in areas where you are most spontaneous and inspired.

Another possibility: we often minimize ourselves in respect to other people and put them on pedestals, and as a result we sometimes inject their values into our life. We compare ourselves to them and think we're not as high-achieving as they are. Instead of wisely living according to our highest values, we unwisely attempt to live according to theirs. In this way, we disempower ourselves: we're trying to do what does not inspire us. We become like a cat trying to live as a fish.

You may also be trying to get others to live according to *your* highest values. Whenever you expect others to live by your set of values or expect yourself to live by someone else's, you're about to experience a state of futility. No one can sustainably live according to someone else's values, because it goes against what's intrinsic to them.

When some activity is highest on your unique set of values, you are spontaneously inspired to carry it out. You don't need to be motivated externally; you're inspired internally, which is why some individuals refer to their highest value as their calling in life, or their métier, or *telos*. (I will say more about the telos later.)

Inspiration versus Motivation

The difference between living an inspired life and living a desperate life that requires external motivation has to do with the congruency between our goals and intentions on the one hand and our true highest values on the other.

If your goals are congruent with your highest values, you are inspired, and you achieve. When you achieve, you gain confidence in yourself, and you perceive that the world is working on your behalf. You're no longer a victim of your history. You become a master of your destiny.

This is the inspired life. When people live congruently with their own highest values, they awaken their inner genius, they escalate their level of innovation and creativity, and they experience their most magnificent and authentic selves.

Your degree of certainty in life is directly proportionate to the congruency between your goals and your highest values. Whenever we subordinate ourselves to outer influences and inject others' values into our lives, we dissipate our potentiality. We scatter and doubt ourselves. We start to think, "I don't know, I'm not, and I can't." As a result, we live with moral dilemmas and internal conflicts. We tell ourselves, "I *should* be doing this; I *ought* to be doing this; I'm *supposed* to be doing this" instead of "I love doing this, and I'm inspired to do this." In the latter case, there's no inertia. Inertia in your life is directly proportionate to the incongruence between your intentions and your highest value. If they are incongruent, inertia and entropy break you down.

Each of the many physiological symptom in our bodies are trying to offer us feedback. Whenever we're not living by our highest value but are attempting to live according to lower, derivative values, we automatically create physiological symptoms. Most symptoms—of any kind—are feedback mechanisms telling you to refine yourself and live more congruently with your highest values.

Authenticity is congruency between your goals and your primary highest value-based intentions. You become the author of your life to the degree of your authenticity. The most meaningful and purposeful way we live is according to that high state of congruency. When we're doing that, nobody has to motivate us; we're inspired from within. We awaken our leadership, we become accountable, we give ourselves permission to shine, and we have more freedom and less constraint from outer authority. When we are not attempting to live according to our highest values and attempting to be somebody we're not, we require outside coercion to initiate and maintain action. The consequent frustrations are life's way of leading us back to what's truly authentic to ourselves, so we can contribute our special work or individual service most efficiently and effectively to the planet. In that state, both our productive service and our rewards are maximal.

In short, if you frequently tell yourself, "I *should* be doing this" or "I *should* be this kind of individual," your congruency may be low. The same is true if you find yourself routinely resistant or indifferent to your work. If you're doing what you truly love, you're much less likely to be resistant or apathetic.

Living by Your Highest Intrinsic Value

Every human being, regardless of age, gender, or culture, is living with a set of priorities, a set of values and objectives that range from most to least important in their lives. That set or hierarchy of values is unique to each individual. (If any two people are identical, one of them is not necessary on the planet.) Each of us is like a snowflake, a retinal pattern, or a voice print—entirely unique.

It's not possible for any two people to have exactly the same set of values, although they may be similar. You may say, "Business is important" or "Family is important," and someone else may make the same statement, but these can have different meanings to different people. Every individual's set of values is like a set of fingerprints, and they are unique.

This hierarchy of values, or set of values, ranges from that which is most important to least important, from that which is higher in priority or value to that which is lower. This set of values dictates our perceptions of the world, because we're filtering our reality through this hierarchy.

What Is an Intrinsic Value?

As you go down your individual list of values from higher to lower, they become more and more extrinsic—that is, determined from the outside.

Your neurosensory input goes through your transducing sensory receptors into the spinal cord, and then ascends up into the brain stem and thalamus, and finally up to the higher areas of your cortical brain. This input passes through the "relay station," or thalamus, where it passes through a value-based sensory filtering process, which decides whether it goes up into the cortex (where you'll be consciously aware of it) or into the amygdala (where you'll have unconscious, impulsive, or instinctive responses). When you are in a survival situation, the subcortical part of your brain fires off, and you're ready for quick impulsive or instinctive, digest and rest or fight-or-flight responses.

You tend to absorb information that you associate with your highest values, you tend to retain this information more effectively, make decisions more efficiently, and you're more likely to spontaneously act. But in your lower values you will tend to be more attention deficit, retention deficit, and intention deficit oriented. This means in the areas of your highest values, you're *disciplined*, *reliable*, and *focused*.

Conversely, you'll *procrastinate, hesitate,* and *frustrate* about what you value least.

Your highest value is that which is most important in your life at any moment. It is the most intrinsic value: your identity revolves around it; it's how you'll identify yourself. You will be spontaneously inspired to act upon it.

The One Highest Intrinsic Value

I emphasize to my students the importance of determining their true highest values, particularly their highest and most intrinsic value, their telos, because it is the foundation of my work and teaching and it is the key to their life fulfillment. My highest and most intrinsic value is teaching in the field of human behavior and self-mastery. I teach seven days a week, sometimes for eighteen hours a day. I'm spontaneously inspired to do it. You don't have to extrinsically motivate me to teach what I love most.

Finding out what's highest on your hierarchy of values, accessing your most intrinsic value, and learning where you spontaneously are inspired to act rather than react will tell you where you're most going to excel.

Although you may not be conscious of it, your life demonstrates what your highest and most intrinsic value is. Finding it out, acknowledging it, and prioritizing your life toward consciously fulfilling it is very empowering, because whenever you do whatever's highest on your list of values, your self-worth goes up, your achievements go up, you expand your space and time horizons, and you give yourself permission to expand and have more certainty. Moreover, your capacity for leadership emerges. I'm a leader in the field of teaching human behavior because it's my highest and most intrinsic value. This highest value is the key to living a highly productive life.

When you're living congruently by your highest value, your blood, glucose, and oxygen flow into your forebrain, and you wake up your executive center, which is the source of your inspired mission, vision, and message. Those who are inspired by a vision have more vitality than those who are not. Those with a vision flourish, and those without a vision perish.

When you're living in accordance with your highest values, you're more likely to be objective and adaptable in your relationships. You're not biasing yourself with superiority or inferiority complexes, and you're more likely to perceive yourself as equal to other people. You're also more likely to love them for who they are.

When you're living by your highest value, you act spontaneously; you don't need to be motivated externally. If you need to be motivated to do what you say is important, then what you say is important isn't all that important to you.

You maximize your resilience and productivity when you live according to your highest and most intrinsic value, because here you're more self-governed, neutral, and objective. When you're attempting *not* to live congruently with your highest values but instead are attempting to live in accordance with your lower values, you become more highly polarized, with subjective bias, and you fear the loss of what you label "good" and you fear the gain of what you label "bad."

When you're living by your highest value, you transcend both "good" and "bad"; being objective, you can see both sides.

When you're living by your highest value, you also tend to transcend ethical labels. You don't judge people; you love them. And you realize that every human being (including yourself) encompasses all of the many human behavioral traits and both of the so-called hero and villain polarities.

You Can Live by Your Intrinsic Value

Your hierarchy of values is changing, either gradually and incrementally or cataclysmically and punctually, and will continue to do so throughout your life.

When I was a child, baseball was important, then surfing was important to me, and now, for over the last fifty years, teaching and writing about what I've researched and learned about human behavior and the universal human behavioral laws has been important to me. Even so, I might have another new highest value evolve in the future.

As I said earlier, your identity revolves around your highest and most intrinsic value. It's where you most grow your knowledge; you become the expert in that area. What's highest on your hierarchy of values gives you a *core competence*, giving you a competitive advantage there.

Your highest value is also your teleological purpose— your most meaningful purpose and inspired mission in life. Your intrinsic value, your real identity, is nonderivative: it's not coming from outside shoulds, ought to's, supposed to's, got to's, have to's, and musts from so-called outer authorities in society. It initiates an intrinsic, spontaneous action.

In your brain, you evoke potentials from outside stimuli that can initiate survival-based, polarized emotional reactions. There are also spontaneous potentials that can emerge from within when your outer perception is more poised and balanced.

When you bring your mind to balance, and have alpha and gamma waves emerge from within your brain, you synchronize your brain and maximize the circadian rhythm potentials in your physiology. You empower your physical well-being and every other area of your life.

Your ontological identity, your teleological purpose, and your epistemological knowledge revolve around this highest value. So do your area of expertise, your leadership skills, your expanded awareness, and your state of enlightenment. That's your identity. That's your true, authentic self, which is evolving and contributing to the world.

Low- versus High-Priority Tasks

Any task that needs external motivation to get people to act is a lower, extrinsically derived value. In the hierarchy of values, intrinsic override and outproduce extrinsic ones.

I learned a long time ago not to lower your value and overall productivity by spending time on low-priority tasks. Fill your day with high-priority activities, and delegate lower-priority duties to others. If a task is high in your values, you'll be inspired to do them. And you'll liberate yourself from what you consider drudgery.

What's higher on your values may be lower on someone else's values and vice versa. You will want to delegate your lower-priority tasks to them because those tasks are inspiring and of higher priority to them, and they will or may delegate their lower-priority tasks to you because it's inspiring and of higher priority to you. This utilitarian matrix, which is called a *relationship*, is designed to help both of you work most effectively and efficiently in accomplishing your dreams. In this way, you'll surround yourself with inspiring people.

External motivation is not a solution for human beings. It's a symptom. It's a sign of activities that are not inspiring—a life of quiet desperation, not a life of inspiration.

Theory X and Theory Y

Douglas McGregor, a professor of management at MIT in the 1950s and '60s, noticed the differences between less productive workers, who required external motivation in their work, and more productive workers, who were intrinsically self-motivated or inspired. He called them Theory X and Theory Y people respectively. With Theory Y people, their job goals and responsibilities matched their own highest values and intentions. As a result, they didn't have to be externally motivated. But people who could not see how their job duties helped them fulfill their own highest value-driven mission required costly external incentives and were overall less productive.

Whenever we act, we do so because we believe that it will provide us with more advantages than disadvantages and more rewards than risks. Every decision we make is based on that premise. Even when we say we didn't act intentionally, we did, because we unconsciously believed that it supported our higher values, regardless of what we may say. Our actions reflect our values more than our words do. Whenever you think you have made a mistake, it's not because you are comparing your action to your own set of values: it can only be due to comparing your action to a set of injected values from some perceived outer authority. The degree that you subordinate yourself to outer authoritative influences and give power to other people is the degree to which you think you're making mistakes. This erodes your confidence and certainty.

For everyone on the planet with their unique set of values, there's somebody with a completely opposite set. What one wants to build, the other wants to destroy, and the combination of the two create transformation, which makes the world work.

The same principles that apply within the individual also apply in social structures: our hierarchy of values dictates our destiny; the collective sets of values within any society dictates that society's destiny. This hierarchy determines how we see the world through our senses and act upon it with our motor functions. It also determines where we're going to excel and where we're going to end up being somewhat deficient.

We have the capacity to excel. People sometimes doubt this innate potential because they have both a habit and a history of attempting to live incongruently with their highest values. As soon as they determine their highest values and set objectives that match, they gain amazing clarity, vitality, and certainty. Why? Because your vitality is directly proportionate to the vividness of your vision. And your vision is crystal clear to the degree that it is free of injected values, which cloud its clarity. Any injected value that clouds out the clarity within the details of your vision becomes an obstacle and a challenge that you will face along your journey.

Someone who knows their highest values and sets goals that are congruent with them awakens a clear vision. You know you have a clear vision if you can articulate it to somebody concisely and they can see the vision and want to be part of it because of the enthusiasm and inspiration that it contains. It's a matter of ordination, not subordination. The most productive leaders and achievers are born and inspired out of high degrees of congruency.

The Limits of Authority

You may have been raised with authority figures. Sigmund Freud, the founder of psychoanalysis, indicated that whenever we inject the values of an authority figure into our life and act in ways that we think align with these values, we'll swell up in pride. Whenever we act in ways that we think go against them, we'll deprecate or beat ourselves in shame, and we will judge ourselves either way. This injected authority becomes the source of our superego, which judges our actions. There's no way out of that prison as long as we continue to subordinate ourselves to external authorities.

There's a difference between subordinating to people and respecting them. Great philosophers knew that the only way out of this prison that Plato called the cave was to have reflective awareness: the realization that what they see in other people is also within them. Plato's student Aristotle also showed his pupils that whatever they saw in the world around them was a reflection of themselves. When they fully saw that in themselves, they no longer subordinated themselves to some external authority; they reflected the traits they saw externally and owned them. Any trait that we see in others that we have been too humble or too proud to admit we have is a power we've disowned. We think that we want to be like our heroes or mentors, but in fact we already have all the traits that they have. We're not honoring them, because they're in our form, according to our own values, not theirs. Whenever we try to live according to others' values, we'll think that there's something wrong with us. We are here to honor our own values.

We become our true, most productive selves to the degree that we have pure reflective awareness and make everyone and everything else ourselves. That means whatever we see in other people around us, we have within us. We're not here to minimize ourselves or sit in the shadows of anyone. We're here to stand on the shoulders of other great individuals through reflection and recognize all of that magnificence inside ourselves. To the degree that we do, we awaken our most productive leadership.

Therefore thou art inexcusable, O man,
whosoever thou art that judgest: for wherein
thou judgest another, thou condemnest thyself;
for thou that judgest doest the same things.
—ROMANS 2:1 (KING JAMES VERSION)

Whenever we're carrying out some activity that is not most efficiently helping us fulfill our highest values, our confidence erodes. That's why the greatest question we could ever ask ourselves is, *how is whatever we're sensing, whatever we're doing, helping us fulfill our highest values?* To the degree that we ask this question and answer it thoroughly, a hidden order emerges, along with certainty.

The quality of our lives is based on the quality of the questions we ask ourselves. Amazing, reflective, and mind-balancing questions awaken true authenticity and create amazing lives. Although we may not yet be full masters of our destiny, we're not victims of our history. In any area of life that we don't empower, we will attract other people to overpower us until we get frustrated enough to empower that area. We empower our lives by asking empowering questions that make us conscious of what is unconscious, which makes us fully conscious and grateful.

That's why we're here to be grateful. Anything we are not yet grateful for is still an illusion—an incomplete awareness. Plato said all learning is recollection. We already have the potentiality, even though we don't recognize it. I don't know what the limit is; I don't think human beings by any means have reached it. Many times, people who come from the humblest setting carry out extraordinary accomplishments.

I recently had the opportunity to work with a lovely young lady who was having some challenges in school. She had a dream, but she was having difficulty seeing how some of her classes in school were helping her fulfill that dream. She excelled at the class that she could see as connected to her dream, but she couldn't see how the rest of the classes were connected to it.

I spent the evening asking her questions and showing her how every one of those classes could help her fulfill her dream. Her energy level went up, her eyes lit up, her enthusiasm came alive, and she saw new possibilities.

As soon as we can see how what we're doing is helping us fulfill our mission, our vitality soars, our empowerment grows, our willingness to receive goes up, and our productivity rises. Our willingness to live an extraordinary life skyrockets. We're destined for that. That is our true nature. Anything less than that is a lie. Our productivity depends on our questions and perceptions.

Telos: The Ulimate End

I call the highest priority in any individual's life their *highest value*. It's what's most important in their life. The ancient Greeks called this the *telos*, which means *the ultimate end or goal*.

Every human being at any moment has a telos. The ancient Greeks knew that this subject was so important that they devoted an entire discipline to it, which is called *teleology*. It is the study of meaning and purpose. The telos is built into the equation of the human experience. This highest value is what we are inspired from within to live. It is, therefore, called an *intrinsic value*, meaning that nobody has to motivate us from the outside to get us to do, or act upon it. Nobody has to extrinsically motivate you to do what is truly highest on your list of values. If you're ten years old and your highest value is video games, nobody has to get you up to play video games.

Neurologists call the end of the brain, or the forebrain, which is the most advanced part, the *telencephalon*. (We've already seen the meaning of *telos*. *Encephalon* means *brain*, so this is the part of the brain designed to work toward the telos.) Whenever somebody lives according to their telos, they are employing this part of the brain. It is maximally developed to the degree that we live according to our highest value; at that point, we have the greatest degree of creativity and innovation.

As you go down your list or hierarchy of values to what is less important and lower in priority, you increasingly require outside motivation to act. This is called an *extrinsic value*: a task that you require outside motivation to do. In a recent article in *Psychology Today*, Geoff Smart writes, "Wondering 'how to motivate employees' is a management fail."

Productivity, as we've seen, is directly proportionate to an individual's congruence with their own highest value. Every decision you make is based on what you believe will give you the greatest advantage or disadvantage, the greatest reward over risk at any moment in time. You will only act if you believe it will provide you with more advantages than disadvantages, and that's based on your telos. Your telos is your ultimate self-actualizing goalpost. It's the pontifical component of your psyche. When you act according to your end in mind as you understand it, you're able to make decisions quickly, and you're able to act upon those decisions and stay with them over the long term. In his book *Think and Grow Rich*, Napoleon Hill said that successful people make decisions quickly and stick to them. That's because they're aligned congruently with their highest value, their telos. Everyone who has a clear mission or telos has a vision and a message.

In contrast to teleology, which has to do with ultimate ends, *technology* deals with means to the end. Technology was the tool that human beings developed to effect the fulfillment of the highest value. With their innovation and creativity, they generated tools and technologies to advance the fulfillment of their highest values more effectively and efficiently—more productively.

An individual's purpose is the most effective and efficient pathway to fill the greatest amount of void with the greatest amount of value, because whatever is most valuable to us stems from the perceived voids in our life. As Aristotle implied, whatever we think is missing is most important: it's a void that needs to be filled. Consequently, whatever is perceived as most missing or void is the determining source and driving force of whatever is perceived as most valuable. If we don't think we have enough money, we seek money. If we don't think we have enough relationships, we seek relationships. If we don't think we have market share, we seek market share. The void drives the value. We want to import it into our spheres of awareness and influence because we perceive they are empty. When we fill them, we're momentarily fulfilled or satisfied. Then, as psychologist Abraham Maslow showed with his hierarchy of needs, we go on to the next need, the next void. Each of these voids determines our values, which determine where we are most to least inspired, purposeful, and productive.

Chapter 2

Finding Your Telos

So far we've seen that your productivity is intimately connected to your highest value. If you are working to fulfill this value or telos, you are much more likely to maximize your productivity.

But as we've also seen, you may not know what your telos is. External influences—parents, society, media, religion—may have convinced you that your highest value "should" be other than it actually is. If you fall prey to this injected value, you are very likely to be less productive and—even more importantly—unfulfilled. Much of the unfulfillment in human life occurs because people don't clearly know their own true highest values or feel that they can fulfill them.

The next step, then, is knowing what your true highest value really is. (When I use the term true highest *value*, I am speaking of your telos.)

Value and the Brain

I've already mentioned the telencephalon in your forebrain, which is inseparably entwined with your hierarchy of values. But there's more. Your brain has developed special cells—glial cells, oligodendrocytes, and astrocytes—that respond to your hierarchy of values. Whenever you perceive actions or events that help you fulfill your highest values, your glial cells will bring nutrition to special nerve cells and strengthen the advanced forward portion of your brain. Your brain is constantly remodeling itself neuroplastically to help you fulfill your highest values.

Your sensory and motor functions are also governed by your value system. We have selective, biased attention and intention. In regard to our highest value, we have what I call *attention surplus order*. If a mother places a high value on her children and she walks in a mall, she will notice children's materials. If a businessman walks in a mall, he will notice business materials. He will not notice children's items, and the mother will not notice business-related items. A mother who has a young baby can sleep through a freight train but wake up at the whimpering of a child because the brain is so selectively biased that it activates and deactivates brain function to ensure maximal fulfillment of values—in this case, the preservation of her baby's life.

This activating system in the brain will respond exactly to your value systems because it's designed to help you fulfill them. Everything you sense and do in your life is a feedback mechanism to maximize your brain function in order to fulfill your highest values. It's not always interpreted that way, but that's what's going on biologically. Your brain is a fulfillment-seeking organism. It's a living entity that's attempting to help you fulfill yourself as an individual, maximizing your potential in life. Because many people inject the values of other admired individuals into their lives, many evolutionary biology scientists have come to assume that your brain is evolved or designed strictly for survival purposes, not for thrival and greater fulfillment. But this is only partly true and depends upon the individual's degree of congruency or incongruency. The greater the congruency, the more *thrival-oriented* the brain is. The less the congruency, the more *survival-oriented* it is. Researchers often select average, desperate, and uninspired individuals instead of inspired individuals for their research, so they conclude that the brain is only designed for survival. But what differentiates thriving human beings from surviving humans is an inspiring pursuit full of meaning and purpose.

Finding Your Purpose

Your purpose is an expression and revolves around whatever you value most in your life. Because every human being lives by a set of priorities, a set of values, whatever's highest on your particular set of values—whatever is most important, meaningful, inspiring, and fulfilling to you—is the center and base of your ontological identity.

Ontology refers to being—in this case, the way you understand yourself; it is who you'll say you are. This is the value that you are spontaneously inspired from within to fulfill, the path of your unique purpose. If your highest value is raising beautiful children, you'll call yourself a mother. If your highest value is running businesses, you may call yourself an entrepreneur.

If you are unclear about what your purpose is, know that it is waiting to be revealed through identifying your unique hierarchy of values, particularly your highest value or telos.

Like thousands of other people I have worked with over the years, you may be surprised to hear that your life already demonstrates your purpose and through the pattern of your highest value(s).

You don't have to look anywhere else but your own life to determine what's most important to you. Your life is demonstrating it.

One basic point: *quit comparing yourself to others when seeking to discover or awaken your purpose.*

People often tell me that they have never managed to be able to find or define their meaningful purpose. In most cases, it's because they are comparing themselves to other people. I'll hear it in their language: "I *should* spend more time with my family"; "I *ought to* work out more"; "I *must* begin investing my money"; "I've *got to* start spending time making friends and extending my social circle."

The instant you catch yourself using imperative language like *should, ought, must, got to, have to,* you can almost guarantee that there's somebody outside of you to whom you've given power and whose values you're injecting into your own. In doing so, you've clouded the clarity of your own highest values, because you're too busy trying to live according to someone else's values and purpose. You're trying to live by others' values or your own lower, extrinsic values instead of your own intrinsic, highest values.

A wonderful example of this was a woman I met during my signature two-day program, the Breakthrough Experience. On day two, she remained completely adamant that she just couldn't uncover her purpose in life. So I asked her, "What do you do every single day that you spontaneously do, that nobody has to remind you to do, that you love doing?"

She replied that she truly didn't know.

I kept going: "Be accountable, and quit comparing yourself to others for a moment. Just answer the question. What do you do every single day that nobody has to remind you to do that you love and that inspires you?"

She shrugged and said, "I spend time with my children."

Now we were getting somewhere.

I asked her, "Do you fill your space most of the time with your children? Are your children frequently around you? Do you spend a lot of time with your children throughout the day?"

"Yes."

"Does it energize you when you interact with your children and watch them grow? Do you spend money mainly on your children? Is that the area in which you are most organized, disciplined, and reliable? Is that what you think about, visualize, and talk about most of the time? Is that what you converse with your friends about?"

"Yes."

"Is that what you study about, read about, and learn about? Is raising your children your long-term goal?"

"Yes."

At this stage, she became quite tearful as she answered yes to each of my questions.

Then I asked, "So what do you mean that you don't know what your purpose in life is?"

She said, "Well, is that a great enough purpose? I think about other women around me, one of whom has three children and somehow runs her own business. Here I am with two children, and that's all I do. It just doesn't seem like a significant enough purpose compared to other people. Still, no matter how hard I try, I just can't seem to motivate myself to do anything else."

"You are not intrinsically and spontaneously driven to build a business yourself because it's not what is truly highest on your list of values and not what is in your heart. You're sitting there and subordinating yourself to this lady you have placed on a pedestal, and you're trying to imitate her. You're trying to be somebody you're not."

I went on to explain how it could be liberating to give herself permission to raise beautiful children because that was her most inspired mission. Her whole current life was pointing her in that direction.

I further explained to her that the mission statement of Rose Kennedy, the American philanthropist, socialite, and matriarch of the Kennedy family, was, "I dedicate my life to raising a family of world leaders." Rose's mission was certainly meaningful, fruitful, productive, and world-impacting. Because of the love you have for your children, who is to say that you could not care for and inspire them to do something extraordinary in the world and make a great difference in doing so?

This dialogue and interaction gives some important clues to discovering, acknowledging, and awakening your highest purpose. You can look at clues such as these:

- How you fill your intimate and personal space most.
- How you spend your time most.
- What energizes you most.
- What you spend your money on most.
- Where you are most organized and ordered.
- Where you are most disciplined and reliable.
- What you think about, visualize, and internally converse with yourself about most that you would love to fulfill and that shows evidence of coming true.
- What you most often converse with other people about.
- What inspires you most and what's common to the people who inspire you.
- The consistent and persistent goals you have that you're relentlessly making come true.
- What you can't wait to learn, read about, and study about most.

If you look closely and objectively, you will see a pattern begin to emerge. In fact, you won't be able to miss it.

What is highest on your hierarchy of values is the foundation of your most meaningful purpose. It is also the secret to your greatest path of productivity.

The Demartini Value Determination Process

What if you're still not sure about your highest value?

To help you find it out, I've developed the Demartini Value Determination Process, which you can use to determine your hierarchy of values, privately and for free on my website: drdemartini.com.

When I was twenty-three years of age and earning my doctoral degree, I came to realize how significant the hierarchy of values was in human perceptions, decisions, actions, drive, and achievement.

I searched for and found various ways of determining what people called "values." But the methods I discovered seemed to be too subjective and socially idealistic—more geared to what individuals seemed to want to believe in, what society expected, and moral hypocrisies than to the actual values by which they were actually living and making decisions. So I began researching and developing an alternative way to more objectively determine values, filtering out social pressure and idealisms.

The Demartini Value Determination Process evolved over the years to what it is today. It consists of thirteen questions that will clearly reveal what your life demonstrates as most valuable to you: your highest priorities or values.

You can go through this process step by step on my website (drdemartini.com), but I will give the details here as well. Just follow the directions. You can write the answers to the questions out in this book, but you might prefer to do it on a separate piece of paper, which you can date and save. Later, you may want to go through the questions again; possibly you will find even more objective and refined results.

1. YOUR PERSONAL SPACE

What do you fill your close intimate, personal, or virtual space with most? What do these items really represent or mean? What are they actually and predominantly used for? According to the study of proxemics, your intimate space is within one and half feet of you, and your personal space is within about four feet.

Items that are not highly important to you are not frequently interacted with and are often tossed or placed distantly in the room, trash, the attic, or the garage. Look carefully at what you have in your closest and most frequented home or office space and see what you display and interact with or value most. Objects that are highly important to you, you will keep in your possession or close by, or somewhere where you can see and interact with them. You may even be wearing some of them—particularly if you are fashion-focused. So look at how you fill your intimate, personal and professional space most.

If you walked into your home or company office space and looked carefully, what would you see? What does your personal or professional life demonstrate as most important?

- Do you see your computer or business materials?
- Do you see business awards, certificates, books, reference materials?
- Do you see sports trophies?
- Do you see design items, paintings, arts, crafts?

- Do you see animals and pictures and books on animals?
- Do you see books and magazines on building wealth?
- Do you see pictures of your children or even your actual children?

Look carefully right now and ask yourself how you fill your intimate personal or professional space. What three items stand out? Keep each of your answers concise: one, two, or three words. Think what each of these items specifically represent to you.

Now ask yourself these three questions:

How do you fill your intimate or personal space most?

_____

How do you fill your intimate or personal space second most?

_____

How do you fill your intimate or personal space third most?

_____

2. YOUR TIME

Look carefully and accurately at how you actually spend your time. What are the three highest-priority actions you spend most of your time fulfilling? You will make time for what is really important to you, and you will run out of time for what isn't.

Even though you may say, "I don't have time for what I really want to do," the truth is that you are busy doing what is most important to you and just don't know it. What you think you want to be doing isn't necessarily what is truly most important and valuable to you. You will find or make time for what you truly consider most important.

Look carefully at how you spend your time. Look at how you structure your twenty-four-hour day. What do you most often do in those sixteen to eighteen hours of awake time? You will allocate your time for activities that are important to you: you will divide up your days according to your true priorities, conscious or unconscious. If a task is not important, you will keep putting it off until tomorrow.

- Do you work ten hours of the day?
- Do you socialize four hours a day?
- Do you read or study three hours a day?
- Do you spend three hours a day with your children?
- Do you spend several hours on shopping?
- Do you work out, do yoga, or train for two hours a day?

Answer these questions:

How do you spend your time the most?

_____

How do you spend your time the second most?

_____

How do you spend your time the third most?

_____

3. YOUR ENERGY

Next, look at what you consistently have energy for and what energizes you most. You will have energy for what's truly highest on your values list. You will run out of energy doing what isn't important to you.

Look at where you feel most vital and enthused in your day-to-day activities. Tasks that are low on your values will tend to drain you, and tasks that are high on your values list will tend to energize you.

- Is it being of service at work?
- Is it solving problems that make a difference in other people's lives?
- Is it working out?
- Is it socializing?
- Is it cooking and entertaining for friends or loved ones?
- Is it shopping?
- Is it reading a great book or learning about what inspires you?
- Is it leading or managing people at work or at home?

When you are carrying out an activity throughout the day that is truly highest on your values—something that you love and are inspired by—you will have more energy at the end of the day than when you started.

Look carefully and honestly at what most energizes you and what you spend most of your energy on. Answer the following questions:

What energizes you most? What do you most consistently find energy for?

_____

What energizes you second most? What do you second most consistently find energy for?

_____

What energizes you third most? What do you third most consistently find energy for?

_____

4. YOUR MONEY

The next determinant is how you spend your money. What do you spend most of your money and your resources on?

You will feel reluctant to spend money on items you perceive to be unimportant. If some items mean a lot to you, you will certainly figure out a way to pay for them. You create or find money for items that are truly valuable to you. You might even be considered to be cheap when you do not want to spend your money on objects that are too low on your priority list. You don't want to part with your money for them.

- Do you spend your money mostly on your home and security?
- Do you spend it on your business development?
- Do you spend it on clothes and accessories for your appearance?
- Do you spend it on specialized education?
- Do you spend it on social activities or events?
- Do you spend it on entertainment?

Look at how you spend your money, or how it is being spent. Answer the three following questions:

How do you spend your money most?

_____

How do you spend your money second most?

_____

How do you spend your money third most?

_____

As you fill in the answers to these first four value determinants, you may find that some of the answers are going to be the same or similar. This indicates that you are on track with this process: you are pretty congruent, and you are consistently doing work in areas that are more important to you. The answers will reveal a clear repeated pattern of your priorities, or hierarchy of values.

5. ORDER AND ORGANIZATION

The next question: where are you ordered and organized most?

Whether you think of yourself as organized or disorganized, you have at least some areas of order and some areas of disorder in your life. You will spend time organizing the items and areas that are truly of high value and most important to you. You will tend to bring order and organization to them. Conversely, you will tend to have chaos and disorder in areas that are low on your values.

Look at where you have the greatest degree of order and organization in your life.

- Do you have an organized social calendar?
- Do you have an organized workout schedule?
- Do you have an organized eating or dietary regime?
- Do you have an organized clothes and shoes closet?
- Are your finances organized?
- Do you have an organized business agenda and management routine?
- Do you have an organized cooking arrangement?
- Do you have organized management of your children?

Look at where you display the highest degree of order and organization. Do not lie to yourself and say you don't have such order in your life. You are not here to compare yourself to someone else who has a different hierarchy of values and in turn minimize where you *are* ordered. Just look for and acknowledge where you are ordered.

Answer these three questions:

Where are you organized and ordered the most?

_____

Where are you organized and ordered the second most?

_____

Where are you organized and ordered the third most?

_____

6. DISCIPLINE

Now we turn to discipline. In what areas are you most disciplined, reliable, and focused? You will be most disciplined in areas of your highest values.

If some goal is important to you, you will be dedicated to achieving it: you don't and won't have to be reminded or motivated from the outside. You will be inspired from within.

Look at the areas or actions where you are most disciplined, reliable and focused—where nobody has to get you up or remind you to do or act.

- Is it your studies?
- Is it your workout routine?
- Is it your social or social media interaction?
- Is it your appearance?

- Is it your dietary or eating regime?
- Is it your business management or activities?
- Is it your family?

Look carefully and be honest with yourself. Answer the three following questions:

Where are you most reliable, disciplined, and focused?

_____

Where are you second most reliable, disciplined, and focused?

_____

Where are you third most reliable, disciplined, and focused?

_____

7. WHAT YOU THINK ABOUT

What do you inwardly think about most about how you would love your life to be that shows some form of evidence of coming true? What three important subjects or objectives most dominate your thoughts—ones that you are gradually bringing into reality?

I am not referring to momentary or transient distractions or self-deprecating thoughts. I am referring to what you most love to think about that is gradually manifesting in your life.

Your mind will repeatedly focus on the subject that has great meaning for you—whatever is highest on your list of values. You may be momentarily distracted by a phone call or a television program, but your thinking mind will consistently return to the area of highest importance.

The key here is to identify what you are repeatedly and commonly thinking about concerning how you would love your life to be, what you would love to do, or what you would love to have.

Make sure the answers to this question reflect the dominant thoughts that are actually and gradually coming true. Do not write down fantasies that are not being realized or not being brought into your reality. Don't write down imperatives, or outer-directed shoulds, ought to's, or supposed to's. Only write down what you specifically think about that you are gradually bringing about; those thoughts that are truly showing fruitfulness and are slowly and steadily showing evidence of being brought into your life?

Answer these questions:

What do you inwardly think about the most?

_____

What do you inwardly think about the second most?

_____

What do you inwardly think about the third most?

_____

8. WHAT YOU VISUALIZE

Now we go on to what you visualize. What are you visualizing about how you would love your life to turn out? Is it gradually coming true? What you most consistently envision and dream about will be in alignment with what is most important to you.

This vision must be showing signs of gradually coming true in your life. Do not include subjects you fantasize about that are not coming true—no delusions or unrealistic expectations, only visions that are becoming reality.

- Do you dream most about your family life?
- Do you dream most about financial freedom and becoming wealthy?
- Is it traveling the world?
- Is it continually expanding your education and wisdom?
- Is it meeting and socializing with amazing people?
- Is it becoming a leader in your field of expertise?
- Is it leading or managing a great business?

What do you visualize about your future life that is gradually, slowly but surely coming true? Write down your three answers.

What do you visualize and then realize most?

_____

What do you visualize and then realize second most?

_____

What do you visualize and then realize third most?

_____

9. SELF-TALK

You inwardly, and sometimes outwardly, talk to yourself about what is most important to you. What do you keep talking to yourself about most that you would love to come true and that is coming true? I do not mean momentary negative self-talk or self-aggrandizement. I mean how you talk to yourself about how you would love your life that is showing fruit.

What are the three areas that you keep talking to yourself about most and are slowly but surely coming true? Answer these three questions:

What do you internally dialogue with yourself about most?

What do you internally dialogue with yourself about second most?

What do you internally dialogue with yourself about third most?

---

10. EXTERNAL DIALOGUE

What do you most often love to talk to others about? When you are having conversations, what subject do you keep wanting to bring it to? What topic do you love to externally dialogue with others about most?

Like everyone else, you want to verbally communicate what is most important to you. If someone discusses a subject that doesn't interest you, you will probably try to change the conversation to a subject that does.

You become more of an extravert when you talk about what is most important to you. When somebody else talks about it, you come alive. When somebody talks about a subject that is not important to you, you become quiet and more introverted, and you probably want to change the conversation to what is more important to you.

If you go up to somebody and they ask you, how are your children? that means that their children are important to them. If they ask how your business is doing, business is probably very important. Similarly with other areas, such as relationships or financial investments.

What do you want to bring the conversation to; what do you want to ask questions about and talk about? What are the three subjects you can't wait to discuss?

What do you most talk about in social settings?

_____

What do you talk about second most in social settings?

_____

What do you talk about third most in social settings?

_____

11. INSPIRATION

Have a look at your life and ask yourself what inspires you most and what is common to the people that inspire you the most.

- Is it great moments of mastery?
- Is it when you or someone else conquers an amazing challenge or fear?
- Is it achieving a meaningful goal?
- Is it when a great leader, actor, performer, or thinker presents or performs their masterpiece?
- Is it when you hear meaningful lyrics of an amazing song?

You are generally most inspired in the area of your life that means the most to you. If you value your children, you will probably be inspired by their accomplishments. If you value your business, you will probably be inspired by your or others' business achievements. If you love building wealth, you will probably be inspired by having your investments grow against the odds, or by wealthy individuals. If you love learning, you are likely to be inspired by learning new pieces of the puzzle of life or by reading about or listening to those with great creative minds.

Write down the three subjects that inspire you and/or are common to the people that inspire you the most.

What inspires you most?

_____

What inspires you second most?

_____

What inspires you third most?

_____

12. LONG-TERM GOALS

What are your most consistent long-term goals? Focus on aspects of how you would love your life to be that are showing evidence of coming true. What are the three most persistent goals that you have focused on and that you are definitely and gradually bringing into reality?

Do not write down fantasies that you are not acting upon and with which nothing is happening. Write only the ones that you are slowly but surely bringing into your reality. These areas have been dominating your mind and thoughts for a long time, and you keep taking step-by-step actions towards bringing them into reality.

What is your most consistent long-term goal?

_____

What is your second most consistent long-term goal?

_____

What is your third most consistent long-term goal?

_____

13. STUDY

What topics of study inspire you most? What topics, information, or knowledge do you seek out in bookstores, newsletters, Google, Wikipedia, documentaries, on You-Tube videos, and from other sources of information? The three answers to these questions will help reveal your highest values.

What do you love to learn about most?

_____

What do you love to learn about second most?

_____

What do you love to learn about third most?

_____

COLOR-CODE YOUR ANSWERS

Once you've entered 3 answers for each of the 13 questions, you'll see that among your 39 answers, there is a certain amount of repetition, perhaps even a lot—a pattern. You may be expressing the same kind of value in different ways, for example, "spending time with people I love and appreciate," "having a drink with the folks from work," "going out to eat with my friends." If you look closely, you can see patterns emerge. In this case, social interaction with friends and loved ones.

Go back through the answers. Take colored markers or pencils. Mark all similar answers with the same color. Do that until all your answers are grouped into color categories.

It is possible that you will have two or more categories where the numbers are equal. If so, mark each one by your order of preference: 1, 2, 3, and so on. If you have a choice between one and the other, what does your life demonstrate that you more frequently choose?

Next, name each category (color group) of answers according to the area of life they show that you value: for example, familial, financial, vocational, social.

Now rank the categories from the largest to the smallest. You can even calculate the percentages: for example, if you have 13 answers related to family, that's 33 percent.

This sequence will give you a clearer idea of what your life demonstrates you truly value—not what you think you "ought to" value.

LIFE SUMMARY

Finally, capture what is happening in your life at the time of doing today's value determination. You may go through this process again on another day and come up with results that are slightly or even substantially different. (As you accumulate these summaries over time, being able to recap what was going on at this time will be of value later.)

Sometimes significant or even cataclysmic events can modify the set of values, either temporarily or in the long term. I recommend doing the Demartini Value Determination Process questionnaire at least quarterly to keep current with your evolving set of values. Your hierarchy of values dictates your destiny. As your values evolve, so do your destinies. Your life's journey is a summation of all of your destinies. As you look closely, you will discover a theme, a mission, or a long-term pattern.

Each time you complete the questionnaire, write short paragraphs, each of which summarizes what is going on in your life in the seven primary areas:

1. **Spiritual:** Your meaningful purpose or inspired mission of teaching for your life.
2. **Mental:** Creating innovative ideas that contribute to the world and using your mental capacities to the fullest.
3. **Vocational:** Global business, career, achievement, service.
4. **Financial:** Financial freedom and independence.
5. **Familial:** Global family love and intimacy.
6. **Social:** Social influence and leadership.
7. **Physical:** Health, stamina, strength, and well-being.

In any of these areas that you don't empower, others will tend to overpower.

- If you don't empower yourself **spiritually**, you may be told some antiquated dogma that may not be rational or empowering.
- If you don't empower yourself in your **mental** capacities, you'll likely be told what to think.
- If you don't empower yourself in **business**, you'll be told what to do.
- If you don't empower yourself in **finance**, you'll be told what you're worth.
- If you don't empower yourself in **relationships**, you may end up doing what you don't want to do.
- If you don't empower yourself **socially**, you'll be told what misinforming propaganda to believe.
- If you don't empower yourself **physically**, you'll be told what drugs to take or organs to remove.

The more areas of your life you don't empower, the more likely you are to feel like a victim of your history instead of a master of your destiny. You'll feel that the world is controlling you and that you are living by duty and not by design.

In my opinion, that's not the wisest way to live.

I believe it's wiser to empower and become productive in all seven areas of your life.

So look at your writing about these seven areas and ask:
- In which of these am I empowering myself?
- In which areas am I allowing myself to be overpowered?

The final step:
List your most recent top three, highest-value driven, most empowered achievements.

_____

_____

_____

List below your most recent top three, lower value driven, least empowered challenges.

_____

_____

_____

If you've followed these directions carefully, you will have a clear idea of your true current hierarchy of values, your areas of empowerment and disempowerment, and your major areas of advantage and challenge, or productivity and unproductivity.

Chapter 3

Accountability and Responsibility

Now that you have some idea of your true hierarchy of values, we can turn out attention to applying it to your life.

The first step is to acknowledge the power of accountability. Most people associate being accountable with accepting responsibility for your actions and taking ownership of what you say you'll get done.

The question is, why do some individuals seem more able to accomplish their aims, while others tend to procrastinate, hesitate, and frustrate?

Some claim that it comes down to your levels of self-discipline. I certainly believe this to be an apparent factor, but I also believe that when considering the cases of high-achieving people, it is wise to look at their highest values to uncover the secret behind their higher levels of self-discipline.

When you do what's truly most important to you, or that which is highest on your list of priorities or values, you become spontaneously inspired and internally disciplined to get it done.

Whether in a personal or professional context, if someone asks you to do what's high on your values, you'll likely get it done, because it's important to you.

However, if someone asks you to do something that's lower in your priorities—something you may feel obliged to do or "ought to" do—you'll likely procrastinate and hesitate. You'll also tend to give up more easily if the task becomes challenging.

You tend to only be truly accountable to what's most important to you: whatever is aligned with your highest values.

You may be surprised to know what happens deep within your brain when you live congruently with your highest values versus when you don't.

When you act in accordance with your highest values, your blood, glucose, and oxygen go into the most advanced part of your forebrain, the medial prefrontal cortex, also known as the *executive center*. This part of the brain is involved in inspired vision, strategic planning, executing those plans, and self-governance. This means that you're automatically more accountable when you're setting goals and objectives that are truly aligned with what you value most. In other words, you become more productive.

On the other hand, when you're involved in an activity that's lower on your values, the blood, glucose, and oxygen go into the subcortical portion of your brain, the *amygdala*. This part of the brain is involved in survival-based, emotional reactions, such as pleasure seeking, immediate gratification, rest and digest impulses, or pain-avoiding, instinctual fight-or-flight reactions. You're more likely to procrastinate and hesitate—impulsively surf the Internet, eat low-quality foods, chat with coworkers, or distract yourself with other low-priority tasks instead of completing your deliverables. In other words, you become less productive.

Let's look at how this may play out in the workplace.

Suppose an employer hires someone for a specific job without first determining whether the job responsibilities are aligned with the hiree's true highest values. In this case, the business will run the risk of hiring a less productive individual who quickly becomes disengaged and is less likely to get the job done.

They may also require continued external motivation in the form of rewards and punishments and micromanagement to accomplish their deliverables.

Contrast this with someone who can see exactly how their job duties will help them fulfill their highest values, loves to perform those duties, and is intrinsically inspired to complete each of them. Such an individual is more likely to be proactive and accountable and less likely to give up when faced with a challenge. (We have already seen this contrast in Theory X versus Theory Y people.)

If you hire someone to do tasks that are low on their values, you're likely to be let down.

Accountability is an expression of living congruently and being aligned with what you value most.

I've already set out my Demartini Value Determination Process. As you saw in the previous chapter, you can go through it for yourself. If you are an employer, I also recommend that you use this process when hiring staff. It will enable you to assess individuals you're interviewing and find out what they truly value. It can be wise to ascertain in advance whether the potential employee can perceive how the requirements of the job description will help them fulfill their own highest values.

If the hiree can't perceive how their specific job description task or action will help them fulfill what they themselves value most, they're unlikely to be highly engaged or accountable. They will probably require reminders, repeated motivation, and even micromanaging to carry out their tasks.

You can apply the same process to yourself. Once you've identified your unique set of highest values, you can ask yourself, "How are each of my job duties helping me fulfill my highest values?"

Sit down and write down your principal job duties or your written job description (which many employers provide). After each item, write a statement specifying how doing it helps you fulfill your own highest values.

If you can't see how your daily tasks are helping you fulfill your highest values, you're less likely to want to go to work and more likely to perceive yourself as drained, frustrated, and distracted.

You become engaged in what you value most. You're only reliable, disciplined, focused, and accountable when it comes to what you value most.

As I said earlier, when you act in accordance with your highest values, the blood, glucose, and oxygen go into the most advanced part of your forebrain, the executive center. When you're operating from this level of brain function, you tend to be most objective, balanced, and neutral. You're also more likely to be more resilient, adaptable, accountable, and productive. You'll tend to walk the talk, lead from the front, and trust your own decisions and actions instead of offloading your decisions onto others, which is the follower's mentality.

As such, you're positioned to become an unborrowed visionary instead of a borrowed visionary, and stand on the shoulders of giants instead of in the shadows of giants.

I've seen individuals make a list of what they would love to accomplish that day, prioritize it, add it to their daily planner, stick to it, and knock it out of the ballpark. This involves saying no to requests that are lower in priority, as well as to opportunists and distractions, and staying focused on what is most meaningful and important to them.

As a result, these individuals have been able to attain amazing accomplishments, be productive, resilient, and adaptable, and go home at the end of the day feeling inspired and present instead of tired and reactive.

I've also seen people choose *not* to take command of their priorities. They're likely to be afraid to say no, to be inundated by unexpected requests, and to spend the day focused on lower priorities instead of what inspires them most. As a result, they are often disengaged, exhausted, unfulfilled, and overwhelmed, while also feeling unproductive and in search of immediate gratification to soothe them.

You might recall a time in your life when you may have felt you were focused on lower priorities and distractions and you were experiencing high emotional volatility. You will tend to react before you think, make comments that you may regret, and spend your days living in fantasy, attempting to escape reality. You tend to feel drained, disempowered, and diminished in self-worth. You may also be inclined to let the world on the outside run your life.

This is the difference between living by higher priorities and living by lower priorities:

- High-priority actions build self-worth and accomplishment. You become accountable and productive; it brings out the master in you.
- Lower-priority actions deplete your self-worth. Instead of being heard, you'll end up becoming part of the herd.

Your identity revolves around your highest values, so the most authentic, accountable, and productive life involves living by priority.

I delegate the responsibilities in my life other than teaching, research, and writing: my three highest values. The top one is teaching, so I spend the majority of my day doing that. Delegating other tasks allows me to focus primarily on teaching.

People often say that I can delegate tasks to others because I have money. My response is that the opposite is actually true: I have money because I delegate lower-priority tasks to others. Consequently, my day is freed up to do more meaningful and productive tasks I love to do, which also bring in more income.

I am certain that it pays to delegate properly. But as we've seen, if you hire someone who's not inspired and who therefore needs micromanaging, that's not real delegation. It's turning a task over to somebody who's uninspired and therefore less competent and who doesn't really want to do it. That's not fair to them. It's not fair to you. It's not fair to the customer. It's not fair to anybody.

In one of my Breakthrough Experience seminars, a young woman explained that she was a qualified medical practitioner who had chosen to stay home to raise her three young children. Her husband worked outside the home for most of the day and returned too exhausted to help out around the house. She was growing more and more resentful about the mundane tasks she performed day after day, although she believed she was doing the "right thing" by staying home with the children.

In essence, she was spending her time doing what she perceived she "should" be doing in an effort to be the "ideal mommy," but she was actually spending her days performing low-priority tasks that didn't align with her true highest values.

I suggested that she hire someone to help out around the house and that she go back to work for a certain number of hours a day. She would earn more per hour than it would cost her to delegate these lower-priority tasks, and she would likely feel more fulfilled. She would also be more present during the time she spent with her children after work and over the weekends.

After applying the Demartini Method* on her infatuation with her mother, whom she had turned into an outer authority and whose behaviors she had injected into some of her lower, derivative values concerning child-rearing, this woman became freed of her internal conflict and went ahead and hired someone to help out at home.

Not only did this become an advantage to her family financially, but she also began to spend more quality time with her husband and children and saw her self-worth go up as a result.

Your accountability therefore reflects how congruent you are with what you value most.

It's unwise to expect someone to do anything consistently and proficiently other than what they value most. If you do, you will probably end up feeling betrayed. Betrayal is not what somebody does to you, but instead what you do to yourself when you project an expectation on other people to live outside their highest values and in yours. For this reason, I delegate my lower-priority tasks to people who love to do them, who will do them without hesitating or procrastinating, and who will probably do them with greater efficiency and finesse than I would.

Being accountable means being able to bring both sides of the human behavioral equation into account.

When you live congruently with your highest values and start prioritizing your life, you have more balanced

---

* The Demartini Method is a systematic, predetermined series of mental questions directed toward the objective of assisting an individual to neutralize and transform polarized emotional feelings into integrated feelings of gratitude, love, certainty, and presence. The Demartini Method is the key methodology incorporated in Demartinian psychology. See drdemartini.com.

objectives; start mitigating anticipated risks with strategic planning; begin seeing the vision of what you would love to do; become more poised, present, and objective; accomplish your goals; and build incremental momentum towards greater achievement.

You also are more likely to experience true gratitude (the forebrain executive center is also known as the *gratitude center*) and see the forces in your life working for you instead of happening to, or against you.

Therefore, identifying your highest values and living by priority is key if you would love to awaken your executive center, become accountable, and live a truly inspired and productive life.

To sum up:

- I do believe that accountability and self-mastery come down to how much intrinsic self-discipline you have.
- How do you expect to live a meaningful life if you're doing meaningless tasks?
- How do you expect to have an inspired life if you fill your days with distracting, low-priority action steps?
- How do you expect to be a leader when you're spending your time being a follower?
- How do you expect to awaken your forebrain's executive function and have governance over your life if you're not living by your own priorities?
- It is wise to identify and live congruently with your highest values if you would love to have a higher level of self-discipline.

- You tend to only be truly accountable to what's most important to you—your highest values.
- When you do what's high on your values, the blood, glucose, and oxygen go into the most advanced part of your forebrain: the executive center.
- The executive center is involved in inspired vision, strategic planning, executing those plans, and self-governance. You're automatically more accountable when you're setting goals and objectives that are aligned with what you value most in life.
- You're most reliable, disciplined, focused, productive, and accountable in areas that you value most.
- It's unwise to expect someone to act in any way other than what fits their highest values. Otherwise, you're likely to feel betrayed.
- Betrayal is not what somebody does to you, but what you do to yourself when you project an expectation on other people to live outside their highest values and in your values.

If you would love to make a greater difference and be more authentic, productive, and inspired by your life, it is wise to identify your highest values, live by priority, and learn to delegate lower-priority tasks. Doing so allows your executive center in your forebrain to come online, enabling you to be balanced, objective, accountable, resilient, proactive, and ever more productive.

Chapter 4

Prioritizing Your Goals

W e've seen that as you go up your list of priorities or values, you become more intrinsically driven, which means that you have a spontaneous inspiration to fulfill them.

As you go down your list of values, with areas that you perceive to be unimportant, you are most likely to need outside motivation to take action.

Think of a young boy who loves video games. Nobody has to motivate him to play video games, although his parents may have to extrinsically motivate him to do his homework, finish his chores, or clean his room.

If a task is low on his list of values, like cleaning his room, it might require the promise of a reward or fear of punishment to get him to do it. But not when it comes to playing his video games: he will be spontaneously inspired from within to do that.

It's the same in the workplace. Some individuals might need extrinsic motivation, like the reward of a paycheck, to get them to go to work every day. They might prefer to spend their time in other ways and therefore need the promise of a reward (paycheck) or the fear of punishment (losing their job) to get them to show up. As a result, they might not be highly engaged or inspired, because they require extrinsic motivation to get the job done.

Requiring extrinsic motivation is a symptom of somebody performing a task that's not really engaging or highest on their unique list of values.

Notice that I used the word "symptom." *Requiring extrinsic motivation is a symptom and not a solution for highly productive human beings.*

But if you fill your day with your highest-priority actions, you automatically increase the probability of engagement and achievement. You'll also be more likely to walk your talk, because you're living congruently with what you value most. Your perceptions become more acute, and you're able to grab more information, take action, and expand your space and time horizons, so you are able to awaken a greater vision of yourself.

When a boy conquers a video game, he tends to want to move up a level or switch to a more challenging game. In your life, this same yearning could be evidenced in feeling inspired to innovate, create, and wake up your genius, because you're pursuing challenges that inspire you.

You'll also tend to have self-governance, because the prefrontal cortex has GABA, glutamate, and N-acetylaspartate: neurotransmitters that calm down the amygdala—

the impulse and instinct center, and the source of your distractions.

In many instances, you may feel driven to perform low-priority tasks because you perceive the individuals around you as more high-achieving, wealthy, intelligent, stable in their relationships, socially savvy, more connected, physically fit, attractive, or spiritually aware. You attempt to carry out actions that you think will make you more like these people, but if these characteristics are irrelevant to your own highest value, you're fooling yourself.

Whenever you subordinate and minimize yourself to somebody else and are too humble to admit what you see in them is inside you, you're likely to minimize yourself, exaggerate them, and inject their values into your own life.

As such, you cloud the clarity of your own true calling and purpose—your true highest value. This highest value underlies key elements of your life:

- Your teleological *purpose* is an expression of your highest value.
- Your ontological *identity* is an expression of your highest value.
- Your epistemological *learning* is maximized in your highest value.

Whenever you subordinate yourself to individuals around you, envy or imitate them, and try to emulate them like a chameleon, you disempower yourself. This is because you're not being your authentic self but are living by their injected values. Most often, these turn out to be lower priorities for you, because other individuals' values are different from yours.

Nobody's getting up in the morning and dedicating their life to fulfilling the highest values on your value hierarchy.

If you don't dedicate your life to identifying your own highest values and living congruently with them, you're sure to be distracted by everybody else's opportunistic projections.

You may have seen this happen in your own life. You may recall a time when you've been infatuated with somebody and were afraid to lose them. As a result, you may have started to behave in ways that weren't normal or natural for you in order to fit in with them and keep them in your life.

When you surround yourself with individuals that you put on pedestals, you minimize yourself. You inject their values into yourself, even though these are not necessarily your own highest values. Consequently, you will likely need continual extrinsic motivation to carry out certain actions or duties at work, because you don't have the momentum-building acceleration of a spontaneous inspired action—your authentic, intrinsic calling and drive.

If you don't fill your day with high-priority actions that inspire you, your day will likely fill up with low-priority distractions that don't.

Lower-priority distractions are the result of amygdala-centered impulses, instincts, infatuations, and resentments, and seeking and avoiding responses to external stimuli. They are based on subjectively biased information, which is a misinterpretation of your outer reality. This includes putting individuals on pedestals with infatuation or putting them in pits by resenting and looking down on them. In the latter instances, you may try to change others to be more like you and attempt to inject your values into their lives. But this is futile, just as it is futile to inject others' values into your own life and try to be like them.

However, if you live congruently with your true highest values, live authentically, and do it in a way that serves other individuals in their highest values, you are now likely to have utility instead of futility. You can also maximize your potential in life because you're more able to create equitable, sustainable, fair exchange transactions with others. Others are more likely to want to have a relationship with you, do business with you, share with you, and socialize with you. At the same time, you are in a greater position to empower all areas of your life.

The path of high productivity and power has a lot to do with priority. If you don't learn how to prioritize and empower your life, you're likely to be inundated with everyone else's expectations. If you don't get up and fill your day with your highest priorities, it will tend to fill up with tasks that aren't truly important but are imposed by others. This outer imposition is a social feedback mechanism to get you frustrated enough to live more authentically and productively by taking command of your priorities.

Entropy, which is a tendency to go from order to disorder, occurs spontaneously in individuals who don't live by priority and put their daily life in order. So prioritize your daily reading and learning, your business actions, your financial transactions, your caring words to loved ones, your social interactions, your physical fitness routines, and your daily inspirational thoughts. If you don't prioritize and empower your life in all areas, you will become over-powered by distracting expectations and intentions coming from others. Living inspired by design is far greater than living desperately by imposed duty.

Fair Exchange

Our self-worth affects what we allow ourselves to be, do, and have in life. This plays a vital role in *fair exchange* of services or products.

Fair exchange depends on your perceptions of the offer and on your hierarchy of values.

Do you think of yourself as generous or stingy? In actuality, you may be considered both generous and stingy, based upon the offer. Salespeople can label you as open-minded and generous when you are receptive to an offer that supports or fulfills your highest values. They label you as closed-minded and stingy when you are unreceptive to an offer that challenges or does not fulfill your highest val-ues. Often these labels are mere projections, emerging in the salespeople's minds when they are ineffective at com-municating what they have to offer in terms of their cus-tomer's highest values or dominant buying motives.

When you believe you are being offered a product or service that is overpriced, you can become unwilling to engage in this assumed unfair exchange. You can awaken a proud, cocky, and narcissistic tendency to retaliate until the exchange is once again fair. The same is true if you believe that you are being offered a product or service that is underpriced. In this case, you can also become unwilling to engage in the unfair exchange. This situation can awaken shame and an altruistic tendency to negotiate back until the exchange is once again fair. But when you receive an offer for a product or service that is perceived to be fairly priced, you tend to be willing to engage in the exchange.

The *equity theory* explains that people innately prefer sustainable and equitable fair exchanges. People raise their narcissistic quotient—they want to take more and give less—when they have received less than they feel they deserve. When someone receives more than they feel the deserve, they tend to raise their altruistic quotient. They want to give more and take less.

Both of these natural negative feedback tendencies help initiate a more sustainable fair exchange. They are innate mechanisms that sustain equitable relations and confer evolutionary advantage. Over time, these oscillating tendencies balance out, so that in reality individuals are neither givers nor takers, but both. When someone with a subjective bias labels another individual as an altruistic giver or a narcissistic taker, it means that they simply have not looked long enough to see the equity that is actually present.

Nature equilibrates any misperceived imbalances through time. When we factor all transactions in someone's socioeconomic network, the equitable fair exchange is synchronously present. But the variables may seem at times to be too complex to allow us to perceive this balance; therefore lopsided labels can emerge and be projected.

Altruistically trying to give something for nothing or narcissistically trying to take something for nothing are both unsustainable and therefore ultimately unproductive.

You, as a miniuniverse, are no different from the greater universe. Whenever you imagine yourself giving something for nothing or getting something for nothing, you temporarily raise or lower your self-esteem.

These elevated and depressed levels of self-esteem oscillate around a mean called your *true self-worth.*

Self-worth = Self-wealth

Your true self-worth determines your self-wealth: what you will allow yourself to be, do, and have in your life.

The more stable, equitable, and centered your self-esteem oscillations are, the more elevated your self-worth becomes.

Indeed your self-worth is directly proportionate to how well you can fairly equalize or equilibrate what you give and take.

The more you give what others love and appreciate, the more fulfilling your life becomes.

The terms *giving* and *receiving* can also be perceived as:
- Giving service of value to others; and
- Receiving rewards of equal value to yourself.

When you give service, it's wiser and more fulfilling to give the service you love and love the service you give. Likewise, when you receive rewards, it's wiser and more fulfilling to receive the reward you love and love the reward you receive.

Goal Setting

We've already discussed the crucial importance of knowing and understanding your own unique hierarchy of values. Now it's time to move to the next step: turning values into productive goals.

When setting goals, it is wise to start with what you know and are certain about and let what you know grow.

In other words, start with what your life already demonstrates that you're currently committed to.

When you begin with what you know and what your life already shows evidence of your already consistently doing and pursuing, and when you set goals that are congruent with that, you are more likely to achieve those goals.

Therefore you are wise to ensure that your goals (intentions and objectives you would love to achieve) and your attentions (what you would love to learn) are aligned and congruent with what you truly value the most. Whatever you value most is where you are highly likely to be the most disciplined, reliable, and focused. They are also where you tend to have the most stamina, perseverance, dedication and commitment. With anything that is lower on your list of values, you'll be more likely to procrastinate, and hesitate. Most times you won't even start, and if you do, you will not sustain your pursuit of it.

Whenever you set a goal that you're not truly committed to—that's lower on your list of values—you train yourself *not* to do what you say, *not* to walk your talk, and instead to limp through your life. This in turn leads to self-deprecation and/or a reduced belief in yourself and less productivity. On the other hand, when you set goals that are clear, certain, and congruent with what you value most, you are more likely to achieve them and increase your self-worth and level of productivity.

Around fifty years ago, when I was seventeen years old, I knew that I wanted to travel the world, so I wrote that down on my list of goals. I knew that I wanted to overcome my learning challenges, so I wrote that down. I knew I wanted to be a teacher, so I wrote that down too.

Each of these goals was in areas where I had already begun to take action; they were not just fantasies about what I thought I ought to do according to some outside authority. Each goal was so real to me that it brought a tear of inspiration to my eye every time I thought about it—another indication that those goals were congruent with my highest values.

I then asked myself, "What are the actions I can do and steps I can take to make those goals come true?"

It's wise to be very specific during this step instead of writing vague generalities and blurred outcomes such as "become rich" and "have the perfect body." Instead, I recommend listing highly specific actions over which you have control. Actually, you only have control over three aspects of life: your perceptions, decisions, and actions. Saying, "I want to have $10 million" is not an action or true goal. But saying, "I'm going to sell this number of items, for this amount, with a profit margin of this amount, with a cost of this amount, with a net profit of this amount, and I'm going to save and then invest this amount in these specific index funds after taxes; I'm going to accumulate this amount over time." Now you have a very specific strategy for achieving your goals.

I didn't reach my goals and become fortunate financially just by holding a vision in my mind of what I wanted to achieve (although a clear vision of what I yearned for was of help). I laid out a specific plan and targeted the specific actions that were congruent with that outcome. Then I automatically transferred specific, progressively increasing dollar amounts to specific investments weekly, so any distracting emotions would not interfere with the strategy I committed to.

When setting a goal, it's wise to start with one you're certain about and to which you know your life is demonstratively committed. This is likely to have a far more productive outcome than wasting your time on wishy-washy or one-sided fantasies, where you try to achieve a positive without a negative, a happy without a sad, a kind without a cruel, and a one-sided life that is impossible to achieve. You are far more likely to achieve your goals when you embrace both sides of your life and the goal's outcome and set real, balanced, and truly obtainable objectives that are meaningful and aligned with what you value most.

An objective is balanced. It's not polarized toward a one-sided fantasy. For example, if I said I'm always going to have positive thoughts and never have a negative thought, that is not achievable. If I said I'm always going to be kind and never cruel, that too is not achievable. But it is achievable to say that regardless of whether I am positive or negative, nice or mean, both are feedback mechanisms to help me move closer towards my authentic self.

Either pole taken on its own—positive or negative—requires an imbalanced ratio of perceptions, which is unsustainable: it is like trying to make a magnet that has only one pole. But if you embrace a goal of acquiring a two-poled magnet, that is obtainable.

As a result, when setting out to clarify, expand, and achieve your goals, it is wise to set up a goal that:

1. Is believable and truly achievable.
2. Is meaningful and inspiring.
3. Is congruent with what you value most.
4. Is a balanced objective that includes simultaneous supportive and challenging contrasts or elements.
5. Is visually clear and has a strategy.
6. Is broken down into specific tactical action steps that will increase the probability of your performing them.

Check to make sure you haven't put incongruent or contradictory objectives together.

In the 1980s, when I was consulting with doctors throughout the United States and Canada, I would have them outline their goals. These often included owning a million- or multimillion-dollar practice while working four days a week, golfing twice a week, spending a certain number of hours each day with their families, and having time for holidays and travel.

When I did the math with them, it didn't add up. In order to achieve their goal of a million- or multimillion-dollar practice, they would need to increase the number of office visits, new patient numbers, or charges per visit. Part of my role was to help them adjust their goals and come up with ones that were sound, congruent, and noncontradictory. As I explained to them, the brain tends to delete goals that are contradictory or mere one-sided fantasies. This is to protect you from the self-defeat and self-deprecation that are likely to result from pursuing what is unobtainable or unsustainable.

Once we trimmed the action steps down to those that were achievable and had a likely outcome, the doctors were able to incrementally take these steps. As a result, their achievement levels completely transformed, and they began to make real progress and build productive forward momentum. Further steps:

Measure your goals. For example, you could look back at the end of the week and identify:
1. What you accomplished.
2. Whether your goals are realistic in practical terms.
3. What this feedback reveals. If your goal was to do X number of calls and you made one third that number, what was the reason? Is this goal truly valuable to you? Is it truly a priority to you? Would you be wiser to delegate it? Would you become more efficient if you linked those actions to one of your higher values? Would it be wiser to adjust the goals or the strategies to achieve them?

Once your action steps are congruent with the goal, you're on track and more able to measure them. You will then be able to see where you are in two weeks, a month, two months, and six months. I love to measure my goals because it means that I am accountable to them. If you're not really willing to apply metrics to your goal, you're probably not truly committed to it.

Ask, what are the highest priority action steps that will lead me to my desired and inspired goal? As I mentioned earlier, you have control over your perceptions, decisions and actions. Setting high-priority action steps and taking those steps is an area over which you have control. You don't have control over the result, but you do have control of the actions that will give you the result.

Identify the obstacles you may run into and how you can solve them in advance. Risk mitigation, planning, and foresight take place in the executive center of your forebrain. If you're planning ahead and looking for possible future obstacles, you're less likely to be broadsided by unpleasant surprises that you could have anticipated but didn't. It is wise to identify as many of these as possible in advance. This can reduce your level of distress and enhance your level of eustress.

Now I'm not negating the practice of visualizing your desired outcome; I've envisioned many goals that have become reality in my life. However, when I look back at what was going on, I saw that that vision wasn't randomly, mysteriously, miraculously, or mystically brought into my life. It was largely the result of the action steps that I was taking and the degree to which the goal was congruent with my highest values and true objectives. I was leading to the probability of that outcome instead of passively sitting back and waiting for it to happen.

Every time you set a goal that you achieve, you tend to give yourself permission to set a greater and broader goal, with increased space and time horizons. As you achieve your goals, not only will you find yourself working progressively faster than you did at the beginning, but you will also build incremental momentum as you go along. Achieving your goals and walking your talk often results in you expanding those goals as you go, so that you begin setting larger and greater goals along the way. It's natural to keep expanding your space and time horizons as you work on goals that will leave a mark on the world—a legacy beyond your life.

To use my own example, I have a goal to be able to contribute to enough people's lives that the work I'm doing, the books I write, and the videos I create will extend beyond my life. There's no limit to the number of people I might be able to reach by doing that. My goal can keep going even though I have a finite, limited time on earth. While your goals start out as mortal, they may end up becoming immortal and your productivity can potentially expand perpetually.

As you face and overcome challenges and achieve more and more or greater objectives, you may begin to reach for the seemingly unachievables—objectives that go far beyond your life.

When it comes to achieving your goals, the so-called labels of success and failure are both valuable forms of feedback. The second you think you're successful, you're *depurposing*; the second you think you're a failure, you're *repurposing*. Both are homeostatic feedback mechanisms to keep you on track, to make sure that you set real goals in real time frames with real strategies.

If you're puffed up, proud, and cocky, you'll tend to set too big a goal in too short a time frame in order to humble yourself.

If you're deflated and down and minimizing yourself, you'll tend to set too small a goal in too long a time frame to lift yourself.

In other words, both are merely mechanisms to help you set real, meaningful goals with real times and real strategies—goals that you'll measure, persevere with, and make happen.

Sharpen your focus by creating a bucket list. Ask yourself, "If I were to die in the next year, what would I love to get done?" Getting in touch with your mortality can often help you think about what's truly a priority in your life. It can also help you set immortal goals for contributions that reach out beyond your life.

I like to ask people how many books they read a month. Many will answer that they read around one a month. If you had a year to live, that would mean reading just twelve more books. Wouldn't that inspire you to rigorously scrutinize each book to see if it was worth making your final list?

Prioritize your goals. Your time on earth is going to go by faster than you think. Make sure you're getting to the goals that are most meaningful, fulfilling, inspiring, and important, and that make the greatest and most meaningful difference. Put those on your bucket list.

When you clarify your goals and align them so they are congruent with your highest values, you will be far more likely to achieve and expand on those goals and live a truly extraordinary, productive, and fulfilling life.

To sum up:

If you would love to increase the probability of reaching your goals and then expanding them ever more productively, it would be wise to:

1. Set goals and objectives that are truly meaningful, inspiring, and high on your list of values.

2. Break each goal down into smaller and smaller daily action steps to increase your probability of achieving each one.

3. Create realistic time frames for each of these smaller goals.

4. Look for evidence of ways you are already making progress towards that goal. If your life does not show such evidence, you may have a fantasy instead of a realistic goal or balanced objective.

5. Reassess your goals regularly in terms of progress you have made. If you are hesitating, procrastinating, or frustrating, you may want to look again at how closely those goals are aligned with your true highest values.

6. Set real goals in real time frames, with meaningful, prioritized metrics.

Chapter 5

Leadership and Management

So far we've focused on productivity in terms of individual goals, priorities, and inspiration. Now we can turn to applications of the same method to working with others, particularly employees.

We've already covered one basic principle: delegating lower-priority items to others who will regard them as high-priority items, because they are in accord with these individuals' own highest values. Consequently, they will carry them out eagerly and with greater competence and efficacy than you yourself would.

We have also seen one way of ensuring that you are hiring someone for whom this is true: you ask them to go through the Demartini Value Determination process, determine their top three highest values, and see how congruent each item or action step on their list of job responsibilities is to their top three highest values.

But there's more to the picture. One aspect is employee engagement: making sure that the employees continue to be engaged and focused on the tasks they have been hired to carry out.

Employee engagement will be one of the greatest challenges you will face in your business career. A century ago autocratic leaders simply issued orders, and subordinates obeyed in response to highly polarized rewards and punishments. Now more educated employees ask, why? They want meaning and fulfillment according to their individual highest values. As a business leader, it is wise to dispense with outdated leadership models and master the art of employee and customer engagement, where respect and equity reign.

Disengaged employees can burden and cost your business heavily. They can stunt innovation, weaken customer relationships, lower team performance, and diminish productivity.

Greater employee engagement requires an effective, respectful and engaging relational leadership method. This includes clarity of purpose, priority, productivity, and distributed power as well as mutually engaging communication dialogues.

Making productive relationships with employees is ultimately one of your highest priorities, because they are the most valuable, value creating, and value sustaining assets you have.

When your employee engagement is above average, you will experience a great jump in productivity. One Gallup poll found that businesses with above average levels of employee engagement reap 147 percent higher earnings per share.

Respect is the most powerful predictor of employee engagement. When your employees feel respected, they become 55 percent more engaged.

When you as a leader are engaged, your words become your actions. Furthermore, you are more likely to reinvest in your employees' learning, mentoring, team building, involvement, and compensation. These areas express employee value and build appreciation, respect, and productivity.

To be an engaging leader:

- You will emphasize a meaningful and inspired mission or purpose that your employees will perceive to be fulfilling and that they, with their own unique highest values, can rally around.

- You will therefore build a team of purpose-filled employees that feel that their own individual highest values are being fulfilled through fulfilling the mission of the business.

- Your employees will be engaging every day in meaningful job responsibilities that fulfill their own individual values.

These are the strongest factors for retaining quality employees today.

Purpose and Meaning

When short-term financial goals are substituted for long-term purpose and meaning, employee engagement and commitment diminish. Employees do not go to work for the sake of a company. They go to work to fulfill what they value most. They desire a career that has meaning.

If you wish to build inspired, creative, engaged, loyal, and committed teams, you will be required to touch your employees and customers in a meaningful way that fulfills their own highest values. This will capture their inspiration and deliver a unifying magnetic pull.

A wise question to ask yourself is: *where and in what way can you contribute to your employees' and customers' lives most profoundly?* The are asking themselves; *what is in it for me to work at this business?* They want to fulfill their highest values for them to be more fully engaged, productive and creative.

Contrary to what many management theorists believe, the primary purpose of your business is not just shareholder value, but also to serve your employees' and customers' interests. In the long run, this is the wisest way to serve shareholder interests. Sustainable fair exchange with all parties is what works most productively in the long run.

Inspire, Engage, and Empower

As a wise business leader, your intention is to inspire, engage, and empower your employees. This will stimulate and distribute energy and empowerment throughout your organization. It is wise to ask yourself: *how can everyone involved become more engaged, productive, inspired, and powerful?*

More fulfilled and empowered people make more powerful business organizations. Conversely, when you become autocratic and overpowering and lose touch with your employee's needs or highest values, which help them become empowered, they stop attending carefully to what you and your customers think and feel is most important.

Increased power sharing amongst your employees is the key to scaling human energy demands. This will ensure innovation, strong customer relationships, and growing your markets.

Contrary to popular belief, you multiply your power by giving a portion of it away. By becoming more respectful, communicative, and transparent, you will elicit the greatest performance and productivity from others.

You can build high-performance teams by being less exclusive and controlling and leading by example. Indifference is expensive, hostility is unaffordable, and trust according to employees' true highest values is priceless.

The Qualities of Leadership

What makes a leader? Is it nature or nurture? Are you born with leadership qualities, or can you learn to develop your leadership skills? I'm frequently asked whether you are born with the quality of leadership or you can develop it.

Some individuals know early in their lives what they're committed to and what's really valuable to them. They're likely to wake up their natural-born leader and build momentum and confidence in that area. For others, this may take place later in life; still other individuals live out their lives without that clarity and leadership positioning.

The Link between Productive Leadership and Values

Having read this far, you already know that your individual set of values or priorities influences how you perceive the world, your decisions and actions, and the areas of life in which you will or will not excel.

Whenever you set a goal or an intention to fulfill what is truly most important in your life, you're likely to awaken your natural-born leader.

But when you compare yourself to other people and think they have more intelligence, achievement, wealth, stable relationships, influence, physical vitality, beauty, or spiritual awareness than you, you'll tend to minimize yourself and exaggerate them.

As a result, instead of living by your own highest values, you will be more likely to inject some of their values into your own life and cloud the clarity of what you feel inwardly called to do.

In his essay "Self-Reliance," the Transcendentalist philosopher Ralph Waldo Emerson discusses how the majority of people conform and subordinate themselves to the herd instead of leading it. As the cultural anthropologist Ernest Becker says, they become part of the collective authority instead of a selective individual authority by trying to fit in instead of having the courage to stand out.

Over the past four decades, I have spoken to millions of people in various settings from prisons to governments, from very wealthy, influential people to those just starting out on their journey. I have yet to meet anyone who does not want to make a difference. And you're unlikely to make the difference you dream of if you're trying to fit in.

Everybody has a leader inside them. Those wanting to grow their leadership skills and abilities and overall productivity will begin to do so once they are courageous enough to be themselves. It is relatively easy to walk on coals or do a bungee jump compared to the true courage it takes to be yourself.

Do you have the courage to be yourself when the world wants you to fit in?

To be a leader, it is essential to stand out, be willing to beat a different drum, and inspire people by exemplifying an authentic life.

The Five S's of Leadership

1. Know what your SERVICE is. A few years ago, I spoke about leadership at a conference of over 1,200 people in Melbourne, Australia. At one point, I walked down off the stage into the audience and began asking people, "So, you're here for a leadership conference. What do you intend to lead?" About eight out of every ten people didn't know!

Know your mission. Those with a mission have a message, and they can articulate it. Those with a mission and a message have a vision, and they can see it. How do you know it is clear in your mind? You can articulate it fluently to somebody else, who can then see it at the same time.

You're not likely to have your greatest fulfillment by earning money without meaning, but by making a difference in other people's lives. If you look carefully, you may well find that the most fulfilling moments in your life occurred when you made some sort of contribution or provided some form of service, receiving whatever you perceived to be a fair exchange. In return, you may have also received tears of gratitude.

So look carefully at what you would love to dedicate your life to. It is not about what other people expect; it is about what is in your heart and what would be most meaningful and what would inspire you.

This teleological purpose or mission of service is an expression of and revolves around what you value most. It is the key to your pursuit of maximum productivity.

2. Gain SPECIALIZED knowledge in that field. As we have seen, one value determinant is: what do you spontaneously love learning? We spontaneously want to learn about what is most valuable to us. It would be wise to learn as much as you can about this area through mentorship, action, reading, studying further, or standing on the shoulders of giants in order to gain specialized knowledge in whatever you are inspired to do.

If you stay focused on what is highest on your list of values, you are likely to build incremental momentum in your purpose-directed achievements. If you have gained specialized knowledge because you love learning about a particular subject, you're likely to become a master of what you do. You will gain respect in that field, which will make you a leader in that field. And this will give you a comparative and competitive advantage, which will add to your overall productivity and output of service.

Whenever you learn about what is most important to you, you tend to absorb the information more fully, because you find it deeply meaningful. You are also more likely to retain information that is meaningful, and you will excel as a result.

3. Learn how to SPEAK out. As I stated previously, those with a mission have a message. So share your message. The ability to leverage your leadership and influence through sharing your most meaningful message is powerful.

Most people are frightened of speaking in front of audiences because they are worried about what others think about them rather than focusing on their service and message. But if they give themselves permission to share that message, they can leverage themselves.

Here are some interesting statistics:

- If you can overcome the fear of speaking, stand up in front of others, and share, you will move to the top 20 percent of the world.
- If you can overcome the fear of speaking and clearly address a mission that makes a difference in your audience's life, you will be in the top 20 percent of the top 20 percent of the world.
- If you can do that and if you can get others to fulfill their missions, you will move into the top 20 percent of the top 20 percent of the top 20 percent of the world.

So speak out. Don't hold in what is inside you.

People who speak out and can articulate fluently and congruently what is meaningful and inspiring to them are unstoppable and are generally the most influential and productive. They are the most likely to be leaders in their fields.

4. Learn how to SELL. Learning how to sell really means learning how to care. This involves learning other people's highest values and dominant buying motives and communicating your own values and intentions in terms of theirs. When you do that, people will tend to believe that you have magnetism and charisma: the ability to articulate what is meaningful to you in a way that inspires and helps them fulfill their mission.

If you help enough other people receive what they would love, you will more likely receive what you would love.

5. Learn how to SAVE and invest. It would be wise to invest in yourself. Until you value yourself, don't expect anybody else to do so. If you value yourself, you will also be more likely to begin to invest in financial assets and have money working for you. You will be less likely to have to work for money as a slave. You will more likely be its master.

- The moment *you* value you, so does the world.
- The moment *you* invest in you, so does the world.
- The moment you have money begin working for you is the moment you begin working because you *love* to, not because you *have* to. The resulting money invested and compounded is now simply paying your way.

It would be valuable to think about saving and investing a portion of whatever you earn, living wisely within your means, and continually expanding your appreciating financial assets.

In short, it would be wise to know what your mission is; gain specialized knowledge; learn how to speak out; learn how to sell and communicate in terms of other people's values; and save and invest. When *you* value you, so does the world.

I am certain that there is no legitimate reason that you can't achieve extraordinary accomplishments and levels of productivity. It doesn't matter what you have been through or what you are going through. What matters is following the principles I've just outlined, which have stood and will stand the tests of time.

The leader inside you may be dormant. This may be the time to stand up and be yourself. The magnificence of who you are is far greater than any disempowering fantasies you will ever impose on yourself. Give yourself permission to stand out, be the leader that you are inspired to be, and maximize your productivity.

Conquering the Fear of Speaking

The fear of public speaking is one of the greatest fears most people ever face. If you understand the actual reason for your fear and transcend it, you will be able to stand up and present a meaningful message to ever greater numbers and sizes of audiences, which could leverage your productivity and brand. When you are able to work through this obstacle, you can go on to pursue many more social achievements.

So what exactly is this fear of public speaking?

It actually has little to do with the fear of speaking itself: people speak fluently to each other every day. It's not even the fear of speaking in front of large crowds, because many have done this at school or in their careers.

The fear of public speaking is actually the fear of speaking in front of someone who we believe or assume has what we don't, or who has more than we have. The fear of public speaking is partly due to the simple law of contrast or comparison.

There are seven primary fears that could be associated with the fear of public speaking.

1. Fear of someone more intelligent.
The first fear is the fear of speaking before those we perceive to have more intelligence. We think they have more specialized knowledge or education than we have.

If you are a high-school student and you look out into the audience and see a prestigious college professor who is an expert on the subject you're about to present, you could have a fear of speaking. Exaggerating them, you will minimize yourself by comparison. You will tend to inject their values into your own set of values and cloud the clarity of your own highest value-driven mission of service, vision, and message. Your speech will become hesitant instead of fluent, uncertain instead of certain.

2. Fear of someone who has achieved more in business.
The second fear is the fear of speaking in front of those you perceive to have achieved more in business.

Perhaps you are speaking on business achievement principles in front of people who have multinational corporations when you've just started your little business.

When you compare yourself to them and believe they have achieved more, you tend to exaggerate them and minimize yourself. When you minimize yourself before others you look up to, you diminish your confidence and withdraw from fluently speaking out.

3. Fear of someone wealthier than you.

The third fear is the fear of speaking before those who you perceive to be wealthier or more financially savvy than you.

If you're talking about how to become wealthy and financially independent, you'll probably feel intimidated compared to those who have already achieved a greater financial positioning, or net worth.

4. Fear of someone more stable in family dynamics.

The fourth fear is the fear of speaking before those who you perceive to be more stable or impressive in their family dynamic. If you were speaking on relationship issues in front of somebody who has a forty-year marriage when you've just gotten married or have had three divorces, you could be intimidated. It is unwise to compare ourselves to others and put them on pedestals. It is wiser to compare our own actions only with our own highest values. If we do the latter, we become more confident in speaking, as well as more productive and influential.

5. Fear of someone more socially powerful.

The fifth fear is the fear of speaking before someone who is more socially powerful, influential, and respected than you. It's more common to listen quietly to those you look up to rather than boldly speaking up. But ultimately, nobody is worth being put on a pedestal (although they are worth being put respectfully and equitably in your heart). So don't be fooled by facades or outer appearances. Everyone has two sides and has strengths and weaknesses according to their own hierarchy of values.

6. Fear of someone more healthy or beautiful.

The sixth fear is the fear of speaking before people you think are healthier and more beautiful than you. When you are talking on health and beauty, you might minimize yourself compared to those you think have more accomplishments in this area.

7. Fear of someone more spiritually aware.

The seventh fear is the fear of speaking before someone you perceive to be more spiritually aware. In this situation, you will withdraw from revealing your inspiring message.

The moment you think others have more than you in any of these seven areas of life, you will tend to withdraw. You become less empowered, fearing what they might think of you. Whenever you assume that others' opinions of you are more important than your own, you tend to draw back into your shell.

You won't be afraid of speaking when you believe you are more influential or powerful than those you are talking to. The fears underlying public speaking boil down to subordinating yourself to those you believe have what you don't. When you minimize yourself in respect to them or exaggerate them, your ability to speak fluently and confidently will diminish.

People combine more than one or even all of these seven fears together when they look out at their audience. They believe some are more intelligent or higher-achieving, wealthier, more stable in relationships, more influential, healthier, or more spiritually aware, or governed.

No wonder they are afraid to stand up and speak.

Realize that nothing is ultimately missing within you. The same talents or skills you perceive in others that you may admire, you have within. They may not be in the exact same form, since you have a unique set of values and display or demonstrate them in your own way. When you discover that whatever you perceive in others lies within you, you give yourself permission to speak out and share your inspired mission, vision, and message more fluently and productively.

Mastering the Art of Speaking

We've already discussed how speaking, engaging your audience, and articulating your message in an inspiring way can enable you to rise up to the top of the world, which can help you have a more meaningful and productive life as well as helping others do the same.

I have been blessed to present between 285 and 426 speeches per year for almost forty-eight years, so this is a subject that I have learned quite a bit about. I would love to share a few insights, practical tools, and tips that have helped me (and others) hone this craft and overcome their fears. I believe that it will help you too!

1. Only speak about what you are most knowledge-able and certain about. Whenever you speak about a subject about which you are not adequately informed and certain, you are likely to feel fear, hesitate, procrastinate, and distract yourself from your objective. You won't be as focused, present, or fluent.

However, if you are speaking about what you're knowledgeable about and you have novel content (or at least more knowledge than anybody in the audience), you are not likely to end up having anxiety about speaking.

Stick to what you know, and let what you know grow as you gain knowledge and as you expand your awareness and skill. It would be wise to avoid stepping outside of your core competence. You learn to play the flute by playing the flute. You learn to speak by speaking and refining your skill.

2. Begin with a story that is personal to you.
This is a technique that Toastmasters International recommends, which they call the *icebreaker*. It is wise to make that icebreaker a meaningful story about your life.

Here's why: nobody in the audience knows more about your life than you. That means that when you speak about your own life, you know more about your own life than anybody in that audience: it is a core competence. And your individual story is more likely to be heartfelt.

If you plan to talk about what you know, sharing a detail about yourself is a great way of loosening up and engaging the audience.

I learned a long time ago that when you are speaking and humbly sharing a meaningful and inspiring story from your heart, your audience members are more likely to go into their hearts with you. I have had 9,000 people in tears together with me when I presented an inspiring moment in my life's journey. It completely leveled the playing field, because we were all there in our hearts together.

My suggestion is to think about the moments in your life related to the topic you are about to speak to, and write down the most inspiring ideas, experiences and stories that are related to the topic and envision yourself repeatedly presenting this to an audience in your mind's eye.

3. Review the section above about the causes of fear of public speaking and see if any of them apply to you. Thinking about yourself and comparing your knowledge to that of your audience will not make you a great orator. Instead, it would be wise to think about:
- The mission and message you want to share.
- How you can make it meaningful, practical, and inspiring to your audience.
- The content you know and are certain about.

4. Have four times the amount of material that is needed to do the presentation than is required in the time you have to present.

In other words, if you have a thirty-minute presentation, have a minimum of two hours of material prepared. I've been using this rule for almost forty-eight years now, and it has served me well. As long as you have more material than you are going to have time for, you will fear less, you will have plenty to say, and you will be more likely to be fluent in your presentation instead of worrying about what to say next and hemming and hawing. From this more knowledgeable position, you will have a greater impact and be more productive in relation to your inspired mission.

5. As long as you speak about a subject that will fulfill your audience's needs, they are likely to be receptive.

You are not likely to make a difference in life just by joining in and saying what everybody else is saying. You can make a difference by finding a subject that is novel and meaningful to you. Take the TED Talks, which are so popular on the Internet. They tend to be original, which makes them intriguing. Find a subject that is out there, on the edge, but involves what you are most knowledgeable about. Present it in a way that meets your audience's needs and fulfills their collective higher values.

Start with your core competence and build outward, focusing on what you already know. If you start with what you know and let it build momentum, you are likely to build a cutting-edge information base and be perceived as a more qualified and reliable presenter.

Remember too that when you can't wait to share valuable information with people, people can't wait to receive it. When you can't wait to get up in the morning and be of highly valued service to people, people can't wait to get your service. When you can't wait to speak and share, they can't wait to receive the powerful information that you have to give.

6. As an educator or public speaker, you have a responsibility to constantly learn and educate yourself. I read constantly every day because I want to make sure that I have new, inspiring information that enables me to refine and upgrade my knowledge as well as my audience's.

It is wise to build up a database of new information that you would love to share with others. Get on your computer and start organizing your knowledge, because organized knowledge is power. Access the greatest and most reliable source of meaningful information available. If you just read some material without organizing it, it is less powerful than if you have it structured with a cohesive and coherent presentation in your mind.

You will make your greatest presentation when you have a subject that you can't wait to share with people and that both you and they truly care about. No matter which group you're speaking to, if you present to them with an enthusiastic perspective, people can feel it. They can tell when you are fully present, and they too will become more engaged and present. That will make a big difference in your presentation and impact. Your results will be more meaningful and productive.

7. Have a cause bigger than any of your perceived obstacles—even if those obstacles include your assumed lack of confidence about speaking in public. When your *why* is big enough, your *hows* will take care of themselves. Write down today why you would love to be able to share your inspired message with your particular audience, or with the world. Then see yourself doing it, visualizing it, affirming it, feeling it, and getting out there and doing it.

Points to Ponder

Instead of letting your fear of public speaking hold you back from making a greater difference in the world, consider the following points:

- Make sure you are fully knowledgeable about what you are going to present.
- Make sure your topic is truly a high-priority topic to you and your audience so you are inspired to present it and they are inspired to hear it.
- Don't let anyone in the audience interfere with your mission and message. Don't let any fear stop you from bringing a message to those you care about. Your fear is simply an assumption that there are going to be more drawbacks than benefits to you if you present.
- Look at using your fear of public speaking to your advantage. In other words, see it as being "on the way," not "in the way." It is letting you know to prepare and to stick to what you know instead of comparing.

By considering the principles and tools I have presented here, you can more confidently achieve your aim. I am certain that you have a message that the world could benefit from hearing. So start learning more, preparing more, and sharing more stories about what is meaningful to you—and watch as your influence expands as a result of your caring and sharing. This will help you become more productive and will help your audiences become more productive in turn.

Chapter 6
Values and the Void

I'm sometimes asked if there is always a balance in an organization between the number of inspired individuals and the number of people who require motivation.

If everybody became a leader at an equal level at the same moment, we wouldn't have an inspired, leadership-based, organizational structure, so there is generally going to be a hierarchical structure; there are only a few ways around it. In any organization, there is likely to be people with varying degrees of motivation and inspiration. The question is, where do you play in the game yourself? You decide where you want to be in the system. Each individual can be a leader in their own niche. You can go all the way to the top by waking up and owning in yourself the traits of the most powerful people. The second you realize that those traits are not missing in you, you get to play on that higher playing field.

When we disown parts of ourselves, we lessen our potential. The *law of the one and the many* applies here. It takes little or no effort to be part of the mass, the herd, the many. It takes a heartfelt, inspired, prioritized, and productive life, following the natural laws of human behavior, to be the one, the masterful leader. But you will have accountabilities and complexities, and it will demand the willingness to be considered and labeled both builder and destroyer. The accountabilities are invigorating and expansive, but challenging. Most people won't face them, so they stop at their own level of competence and endurance.

Sometimes we become so engrossed in a business that we forget its real purpose: to serve or fill the needs of other human beings. The more people whose needs we can fill, the more earning potential we have. Our purpose is to serve people by fulfilling their highest values or greatest needs and in turn sustainably fulfill our own.

If you're dedicated to serving somebody else's needs but you're not inspired by that service, it can even be a hindrance. How many people have we seen that are uninspired by their careers, even though they make decent money? They're serving a need, but they're not feeling fully served themselves, and there's something perceptually missing inside them. They stay in their jobs unfulfilled. They perceive that they have the Monday morning blues, the Wednesday hump days, the thank God it's Fridays, and the week freaking ends. This attitude can often be due to unrealistic comparisons with others or with other jobs assumed to be more fulfilled or fulfilling.

In a store, employees who are not inspired about delivering quality service hinder the transactions. Therefore it is essential to have fair exchange and maximize fulfillment on both sides of the equation. Otherwise future potential business productivity and transactions are diminished.

Business started out thousands of years ago with exchanges between human beings, and even today business is still about transactions between human beings. The vehicles and technologies have changed, but the core construct is the same.

Sustainable fair exchange means that you've maximized the fulfillment of both parties' highest values. If you sell a product to somebody that doesn't really fill their needs, or your selling that item doesn't really fulfill your own needs, eventually those transactions will wane. There will either be a turnover in clients on the one hand or in the job position on the other. Trying to give something for nothing, or trying to get something for nothing is in the long-term nonproductive and unsustainable.

Notice also that in the hierarchy of jobs, you often have a higher turnover rate in the lower socioeconomic positions than you do in the higher positions. Thus there's commonly more volatility in the lower echelons in society. This fact reflects another aspect of the law of the one and the many. As you approximate the highest levels, you have one, and as you go down to the lower levels, you have a turnover of many. You see the same principle in anthropology. In the lower socioeconomic levels, you have a higher fertility and mortality rate; in the higher socioeconomic levels, you have a lower fertility and mortality rate.

We could say that the level of the one is more stable and fixed and the level of the many is more unstable and variable. One is more lasting, and the other less lasting. At the higher level, there is a higher probability and degree of fair exchange. At the lower level, there is a higher probability and degree of *unfair* exchange. When there's a less than fair exchange, either the client disappears or the individual serving disappears. Hence the volatility at the lower levels. An individual who is doing an unsatisfying routine job, which requires continual extrinsic motivation in the form of rewards and punishments to do the bare minimum, is more likely to quit than one who is productively doing a job that is more intrinsically inspiring and congruent with their highest values.

How, then, can we maximize long-term relationships with clients? And how can we maximize long-term focus in business? You've heard that immediate gratification can cost you money and long-term vision and deferred gratification can pay you money. The majority of aspiring day traders on the stock market either don't make or don't keep much money; only a few percent do. People with longer-term visions are much more patient and achieving, like Warren Buffett or Benjamin Graham, the father of value investing. In real estate, if you flip properties in and out, you're less likely to make or hold on to money than if you're willing to stay in for a period of time, usually at least one to three economic cycles.

Business as Human Behavior

Now let's apply these principles to human behavior, because business is human behavior, and whoever has knowledge and skills about human behavior is going to have a business advantage over someone who doesn't.

Your top priority in business is mastering human skills: dealing with management of people. In a sales process, it is wise and more productive to find out the prospect's highest values or needs and communicate your sales offer in terms of those needs. In the same way, when you're inspiring teams, it is wise and more productive to find their highest values and needs, because nobody ever goes to work for the sake of a company; they work to fulfill what they value most. Moreover, nobody buys a product merely because they're loyal to a company; they buy because the product fulfills a value, a need in their life; it fills a void. Nobody creates a company purely for the sake of altruism; they also do it to fulfill their own higher values.

Let's look a little more into values. *Axiology* is the study of values and worth. It is, I believe, the most important ology that anybody will ever study in their life. Although it is the most crucial of all disciplines, it is one of the least studied. Why? I don't know the exact reason. Even so, I think it would be prudent to make it one of the first studies from elementary school all the way up, because it is the cornerstone of human behavior, and all our actions revolve around it.

As we've seen, everybody has a set of priorities. As we've also seen, I call the highest priority in any individual's life the *highest value*. As we've seen, the ancient Greeks called this the *telos*: the ultimate end. Teleology is the study of this ultimate end, of meaning and purpose. The telos is built into the equation of the human experience.

This highest value is what we are spontaneously inspired from within to fulfill and live. It is therefore called an *intrinsic value*, meaning that nobody has to motivate us from the outside to do it; our ontological identity revolves around it. Nobody has to motivate you to do what is truly highest on your value.

As you go down the list of values to what is less important and lower in priority, you increasingly require outside motivation to act. This is called an *extrinsic value*: a task that you require outside motivation to do. This value is your deontological or dutiful identity and is created out of socially driven disowned parts.

Maximum productivity, as we've seen, is directly proportionate to an individual's congruence with their own highest value. Every decision you make is based on what you believe will give you the greatest advantage over disadvantage, the greatest reward over risk at any moment in time. You will only act if you believe it will provide you with more advantages than disadvantages, and that's based on your hierarchy of values and telos. Your telos is your ultimate or transcendent decision maker, or action initiator. It's the pontifical component of your psyche. When you act according to your end in mind as you understand it, you're able to make decisions quickly, and you're able to act upon those decisions and stay with them over the long term. In his book *Think and Grow Rich*, Napoleon Hill said that successful people make decisions quickly and stick to them. That's because they're aligned congruently with their highest value, their teleological purpose. *Your highest value* is another name for your mission or purpose in life. Everyone with a clear mission, a telos, has a vision and a message.

Your telos is your end in mind. Technology is the means to that end. Technology is the tool that human beings developed to fulfill their highest values. With their innovation and creativity, they generated tools and technologies to advance the fulfillment of their highest values more effectively and efficiently.

An individual purpose is the most effective and efficient pathway to fulfill the greatest number of voids with the greatest amount of value, because whatever is most valuable to us stems from the underlying, judgment-based voids that we have subconsciously stored in our minds. As Aristotle said, whatever we think is most missing becomes most important: it's a perceptual void that we yearn to fill. Consequently, the greatest void is the source of the greatest value. If we don't think we have enough money, we seek money. If we don't think we have enough relationships, we seek relationships. If we don't think we have market share, we seek market share. Our voids drive our values. They consist of what we perceive to be most important because we perceive it to be most missing; it is where we are feeling the most emptiness. When we fill it, we feel satisfied or fulfilled. Then, as Maslow showed with his hierarchy of needs, we go on to the next need, the next void. Our degree of productivity correlates with our degree of effective and efficient fulfillment.

Values and the Brain

Your telencephalon, particularly the executive center of your forebrain, is so entwined with your highest values that they're inseparable. In fact, your brain has developed special cells—glial cells, oligodendrocytes, and astrocytes—that respond to your value systems. Whenever you see something that supports your highest values, and whenever you do something that helps you fulfill these values, your glial cells will bring nutrition, growth factors, and myelination to the nerve cells and strengthen your forebrain. Your brain is neuroplastically remodeling itself to help you fulfill your hierarchy of values.

Our sensory perceptions and our motor actions are also governed by our value system. In regard to our highest value, we have what I call *attention surplus order*. We have selective, biased attention. As I've said, if a mother places a high value on children and she walks in a mall, she will notice items related to children.

The reticular activating system (RAS) in your brainstem will respond exactly to your hierarchy of values, because it's designed to help you fulfill them. Everything you sense and do is a feedback mechanism to maximize your forebrain function so that you can fulfill your highest values. It's not always interpreted that way, but that's what's going on biologically. Your brain is a fulfillment-seeking organism. It's a living entity that's attempting to help you fulfill yourself as an individual, maximizing your potential. Because most individuals are unclear about their hierarchy of values and what is truly most important in their lives, scientists perceive their brains to be only survival-oriented.

I've said that in order to have a successful business, it is essential to maintain sustainable fair exchange between your values and those of your employees, stakeholders, shareholders, and customers. The laws of business management support this principle. If you are not fulfilling your highest values in your career, you have a high probability of being distracted, disengaged, and unproductive. If you're not fulfilling the highest values of your clients because you have a short-term view of them, this will affect the health and wealth of your business. That's why making a quick sale is generally not as valuable as developing a long-term caring relationship with clients. You've heard (rightly) that it costs more to get a new client than it does to keep one.

How do we maximize the fulfillment of our highest values in business? How do we maximize the fulfillment of our clients' and our employees' highest values? When we can accountably answer those questions, we can maximize our productivity, profitability, and meaningfulness.

If you know what your highest values are and you're willing to create a career to fulfill them, you have the highest probability of a sustainable career. If you're in a career that you do not see as fulfilling your highest values, you will have a high probability of moving around, with less fulfilling short-term careers.

Companies recognize this fact. They want to know your job history. If they see you popping in and out of jobs every three months, they're likely to conclude you haven't found yourself, you don't know yourself, and you're probably going to be flighty. But if you have a long track record of one focus and mastery of that focus, you have a higher probability of being wisely selected and productive. A company wants to know that when they hire you.

Are you seeing how these facts tie together with some of your practical business activities? Fulfillment in business is directly proportionate to the void-value axis of each individual. If you have a great driving void to fulfill in an area of expertise, you'll be more likely to offer a great value in that area.

The Void in Personal Life

Let me give you an example of a void in my own individual life. When I was a child, I was told I would never read, write, or communicate, never amount to anything, and never go very far in life. I dropped out of school. I lived on the streets, I didn't fully read until I was eighteen. I had a void there. I discovered that void and concentrated on filling it. (Similarly, you'll see that famous doctors often had health issues in their or their family's lives.)

I also had a secondary void. At one point I was challenged by strychnine poisoning, which damaged my neuromuscular system. This drove me toward studying natural health care approaches, particularly chiropractic, the study of neuromuscular skeletal concerns. My void became a value. If you identify the greatest void in your life, you will find where you have the greatest depth of drive.

Many years ago, I was consulting with a wood, forestry, and paper company in Melbourne, Australia. First I met with the four key executives. At this point, the company was losing market share to Asian competitors. The executives were concerned that the company's founder, who was around sixty-three, was waning in his drive, knowing he was about to retire, and was no longer focusing intently on the business. They wanted him either fired up or out so they could take over the company and move it forward, but they couldn't tell him to leave, because he still led the company.

Finally, I met the founder and confronted him with a simple question: "Tell me what you feel is going on in your business. I just want to hear what you have in your perception."

He started giving excuses. Whenever you see excuses, you know someone is distracted and dissociated from their chief aim. He said, "We can't compete with the Asians because of labor costs," and so on.

I said, "Now that you've got that off your chest and we've got the bullshit out of the way, I want to ask you a deeper question. What inspired you, or made you decide, to start this business?" (It is not wise to forget the core reason you initially formed a business.)

The CEO leaned back in his chair. He wasn't expecting that question. He said that as a little boy, he came from a family living in poverty. At the time, a kind of desegregation was occurring in the country, and the government started busing less fortunate and impoverished children to the same schools as the wealthy children. He ended up going to a school with children from wealthier families, but he was one of the poorest children in the school. He went the first day to class and saw that everybody else had plenty of paper to write on, but his parents couldn't afford it. He was the only one that didn't have enough money to buy paper. At the end of the day, when everybody went home, he went to the school trash cans, pulled out partially used paper, and took it home. He trimmed the paper, made his own pads, and glued them together. As weird as that may sound, when you're impoverished and somebody else has a possession that you don't, that's important, because you don't want to feel inferior or rejected.

At that time, this man had a void, a perceived pain in his life. He was feeling humiliated, and he didn't like to see people like him stuck with that. Eventually, as he started to speak about this with me, tears came to his eyes, and he said he wanted to make sure that children like himself had paper. That was his purpose. He wanted to bring paper to the children that didn't have paper.

This man's void drove his values: he wanted to bring paper first to children and then to the world. As usually happens, when he started his business, there was a lot of innovation, creativity, and drive. Once you get to be a big business, the speed of growth sometimes slows down: it's hard to bring in innovation, because you can't double a $1 billion business as easily as you can a $10,000 business. So he started slowing down. He went through the trials and tribulations of management, the hiring, the firing, the marketing, the setbacks, the economics—the responsibilities that became more complex and more tedious as he grew the business and started to lose sight of his original inspired vision.

This man temporarily lost sight of his original purpose. I know that's a cliché in business circles, but it is more significant than that. Much of the corporate rubbish called "purpose statements" has practically no meaning whatsoever. It's marketing verbiage that has little to nothing to do with the seller or the customer. In order to have meaning and productive power, a purpose statement has to hit heartstrings.

I noticed that while this CEO was saying this, he was teary-eyed. The other executives who were there were somewhat overwhelmed, because they had never heard this story, and they were brought to tears also.

"So," I asked, "you've basically been waning in your business mission focus and getting ready to retire. Did you forget the children?"

That got to him, and he said, "I guess I did."

"Is that really how you want it to wind down?"

"No."

"Why are you retiring?"

That day after being confronted by that question, the CEO decided to get back to focus. The other executives didn't truly want him to leave, they just wanted him to be inspired, although they were willing to take over if he wouldn't. In three months, he had new marketing and a new focus, and over the next six months, productivity rose, so market share increased. Market share has a lot to do with the leader's degree of congruency: the greater the congruency, the greater the drive, the greater the inspiration, and the greater the discipline, reliability, and focus.

Language and Congruency

You identify yourself with whatever's highest on your list of values; you disown whatever's low in your values. From now on, listen carefully to the people in your business: their language will reveal their degree of congruency. If they say, "The company *I work for*," they're a bit dissociated. If they say, "*My* company," they're more associated. If they communicate an identity between themselves and the company, they have a high degree of congruency between their job description and their highest values. If they see the relation in a distant or dissociated way, you'll hear the dissociation in the language. They'll say, "The company I work for," as if it's out there, away from them; they don't own or identify with it. Whatever is lower on their list of values, they keep distant from themselves—including their own position within the company. Whatever is highest on their list of values they keep close to themselves, physically and metaphorically.

Your degree of ownership is to the degree of your congruency with your highest values. In areas that are low on your value list, you tend to have attention deficit disorder, retention deficit disorder, and intention deficit disorder, instead of attention surplus order, retention surplus order, and intention surplus order.

You tend to absorb, remember and apply what is valuable to you. If you meet somebody that's very important to you, you'll tend to remember their name. If you meet somebody that you think is of zero importance, you won't remember their name the moment after they said it.

In education, learning retention is directly proportionate to the relation between the topic, class, or curriculum and the student's highest values. If they can see how the topic, class, or curriculum is helping them fulfill those values, they'll absorb, retain, and apply the information. If they see no relationship between the curriculum and their values, they'll only pass the test with short-term memory to get it over with.

You may have been frustrated by teaching the same lesson to the same people in a company over and over again. They don't seem to retain information. You seem to just keep reminding them and extrinsically motivating them. That is a symptom of incongruence between their job description and their highest values. How much does that cost companies? The overhead and the cost of business go up as the congruence goes down. By contrast, expectancy, efficiency, priorities, performance, and overall productivity go up along with high congruency.

So it is wise to identify your highest value and the void driving you to drive your company. If you align the niche of your business to your highest value and void, you will have a higher probability of building business momentum and overriding inertia. You will also more effectively build brand recognition, which is less likely to occur if your highest values are unfulfilled.

Let me give you another example of how achievement emerges from filling a profound void. I once had the opportunity to speak at a conference in Vienna. Another speaker was the British geneticist Paul Nurse, who had received a Nobel Prize for his studies of genetics, proteins, and cell division and the origin and development of life. From a young age, he was driven to know how life began and evolved.

When Nurse was getting his Nobel Prize, the selection committee asked him for a complete biography. As he was pulling it together, he discovered a fact he hadn't known: his real mother pretended to be his sister, who had illegitimately gotten pregnant at a young age. Her parents partly covered up the illegitimacy and kept his real mother in Norfolk, England, and they lived and raised him in London. His grandmother and grandfather took Paul and raised him, making him believe that they were the mother and the father. Nurse did not really know his real mother was his sister. He only found this out when he acquired a birth certificate.

As a result of this background, there was apparently inside Nurse a thirst to discover the origin and development of life—his own life—because if you regress a child prior to birth, you will discover that they have knowledge that many people don't realize. Nurse's feeling of a void in regard to his own origin drove him relentlessly to pursue his inquiry to the point of winning a Nobel Prize.

Another example: Sir Isaac Newton's father died before he was born. His mother, who was young, felt she had to find a new husband with adequate means, so she had to give her son up temporarily. Newton grew up with a void of father and mother. He had a relentless quest to know Mother Nature and to know the will of God the Father. In order to know the divine master plan, he became a driven student of religion and natural philosophy. At one point, that void, combined with the bubonic plague, drove him to spend two years isolated in a room—only eating and reading, and seldom if ever leaving.

Our greatest void can become our greatest value: our telos. Accessing that to the degree of high congruency will determine your degree of leadership. Your leadership capacities are innate, and they are directly proportionate to your degree of congruency. Everyone has a leader inside them. If you're congruent, you will awaken to your leadership capacities. The greater the congruency, the greater the capacity for leadership.

As the stories of both Paul Nurse and Isaac Newton suggest, the difference we want to make in the world often reflects the unfulfilled parts or voids of ourselves. You may be assuming that you want to make a difference in a general sort of way. But if you look into your psyche and probe into the mysteries of your own being, you will discover that the actual difference you want to make stems from your greatest void. You primarily want to make a difference that represents parts of yourself that you haven't filled.

Some psychologists experienced incest as children and have ended up specializing in incest because of their perceptions of their experiences. Others who were beaten go on to specialize in battering issues due to their perceptions. Many sports figures had difficulties with health and/or physical activities.

I was born with a speech and learning disorder and an inwardly rotated left arm and leg. Once I got out of my arm and leg braces, that led me to want to be free and excel in running and throwing, which drove me to excel in baseball. After building momentum and notoriety as a young baseball player in Houston by age twelve, my parents moved to Richmond, Texas, a lower socioeconomic area, which had a lot of gangs and drugs and a disorganized baseball league. After I had struck out a certain batter while I was pitching, I would be attacked, beaten, and injured with chains and knives by a gang leader or member who was a sibling or friend of the batter. So I withdrew from baseball and went into a second sport that required the use of my arms and legs: surfing. Later, at age seventeen, I had a brush with death (strychnine poisoning), which led me to my second most significant void: speaking and learning, which moved me to overcome my learning challenges and return to school and academics.

Our hierarchy of values dictates our destiny. Our hierarchy of voids dictates our hierarchy of values. The greater the void, the greater the value. The greater the value, the greater the drive. The greater the drive, the greater the purpose. The greater the purpose, the more momentum and leadership we will have—if we find that purpose and act consistently and congruently towards it.

The Wisdom of the Universe

I'm a believer in an information-filled universe—what some might call an intelligent universe—and I have accumulated mathematical and astrophysical evidence to support this belief. As Albert Einstein said, "It is enough for me to contemplate the mystery of conscious life perpetuating itself through all eternity, to reflect upon the marvelous structure of the universe which we dimly perceive, and to try humbly to comprehend an infinitesimal part of the intelligence manifested in nature."

I believe the wisdom of the laws of the universe, particularly as they relate to human behavior, ensures that when you're not living according to your highest values, you create or attract frustrations and distractions. You create signs and symptoms in your life until you grow frustrated enough to say, "I deserve more than this. I want to live according to my highest values," which is more objective and in line with the universal laws of intelligent symmetry.

The world is offering you feedback and lovingly helping you to be authentic. The most authentic you is your identity, which is an expression of your highest value. You automatically increase the probability of rising in socioeconomic position to the degree of your congruency with your highest values.

If you set a goal that is congruent with your highest values, with your more balanced state of mind, you will be more able to endure greater levels of pain and pleasure in the pursuit of it. You'll walk your talk; you won't let yourself down. But if you attempt to pursue a goal that's aligned to your lower values, you won't walk your talk; you'll limp your life, and your productivity will subside.

When a leader or manager of a company invests in an employee, they prefer to have somebody that walks their talk. We call that *integrity*. Integrity means that your intentions and your highest values are one and the same. Integrity means integration. You're integrated; there's nothing missing in you. With integrity, once you've achieved one goal, you tend to set a greater one. We have goals; we achieve them. We set greater and larger goals; we achieve them. The goals continually grow until we set ones that are beyond ourselves. Goals move from those in concrete space and time to ones that become abstract, spaceless, and timeless—lasting beyond one's life.

We yearn to create immortal goals, which eventually create legacies that live beyond our own mortal lives. People who live according to their highest values have a high probability of leaving a legacy for generations to come. Their productivity continues beyond their life through the impact that they have made. The Roman philosopher, politician, and poet Seneca said that you are not here to act for your own generation, but for generations to come

Those who have the greatest vision leave the greatest effect. Individuals are measured by their most distant ends. If you're living merely for immediate gratification, you will not make the same difference as you will if you set goals that pass through and beyond your life. People who are not congruent do not build momentum or have expanded space and time horizons. They generally have higher turnover rates in their jobs. They live in survival and security instead of self-actualization and inspiration.

Time horizons vary with different levels of society. The factory worker lives thinking from day to day; the CEO thinks in terms of decades or generations. The sage thinks in terms of centuries or millennia. To the degree that we live according to our telos, we automatically expand our space and time horizons, and we hold on to the vision that is most meaningful and inspiring to us. We will persist with a long-term vision to accomplish our objectives and will produce more masterfully.

Masterful individuals are congruent. They know themselves. They love themselves. They *are* themselves. The less masterful masses usually live in short time frames of immediate gratification. The master delegates objectives within appropriate time and space horizons and assigns appropriate degrees of accountability and complexity. The master also communicates according to the highest values of the individuals they lead.

Schopenhauer is quoted as saying that we become ourselves to the degree that we make everyone else ourselves. That means we have whatever we see in other people, and we are wise to acknowledge it within us. The wisest CEOs know that whatever they see within the individuals within their companies is a reflection of themselves. Those that function from their subcortical brains have a lower capacity for such reflection. They fail to see that both what they admire and what they despise in others are in themselves. At the lowest rungs of leadership awareness, there's a lot of judgment, emotion, and volatility. These emotionally reactive individuals may go to a soccer game and watch other people perform exceptionally well, but they won't perceive themselves capable of playing, because they do not or cannot see the same capacities within themselves. They have deflective awareness rather than reflective awareness. Individuals at the top, with a higher reflective awareness, are more likely to participate in or even own the soccer team instead of being mere spectators.

Nature does not throw away old mechanisms; it builds new layers on top of them through a modified form of recapitulation. Although you may have started at the bottom rungs of a company, when you become the master and leader, you will remember where you started and how you mastered the art of high-value communication with those you lead along the way.

A Congruency Quiz

Here is a short quiz to help you to determine and enhance your congruency.

Write down ten activities you do in your business or work every day.

1. _____
2. _____
3. _____
4. _____
5. _____
6. _____
7. _____
8. _____
9. _____
10. _____

Then rank these in degrees of fulfillment on a one to seven scale, seven being highly fulfilling, one being unfulfilling. Seven means, "I can't wait to get up in the morning and do that." One means, "I hate doing that and feel I have to do it out of duty or obligation."

Now wherever you have a level one or a two, right next to it write, "In the way." Anywhere you have a six or a seven, write down, "On the way." When you rank an activity at seven, you perceive it as congruent with your highest values: it's helping you fulfill what is most important to you, so you see it as on the way.

If you list most of your tasks as five, six, or seven, you are likely to have congruency between your job responsibilities and your highest values. If you rank most of your tasks at one, two, or three, there may be considerable discrepancy between the daily work activities you do and your highest values. The greater the discrepancy, the less the probability of great productivity.

Values, Communication, and Selling

Wise and masterful leaders can see the links between their own highest values and those of their executives and employees. If a leader is not communicating what they want done in terms of their executives' or employees' highest values, it is very likely that they will not communicate those values to their customers. A leader's actions can be reflected throughout the entire company. If the individual at the top can master the skill of communicating respectfully in terms of the employees' highest values, that will percolate down to the managers, down to the workers, all the way down to the clients or customers. After all, you won't sell exceptionally well unless you can show the customer how your product, service, or idea matches their dominant buying motive or highest value. If you don't know how to do that or if you don't know what your customer's highest values are, you will automatically run into customer resistance. The customer will see you as in the way, not on the way. They'll see you careless, not caring.

When you're selling to a customer, you begin by introducing yourself and establishing rapport. After establishing rapport, you establish a need, which determines their voids, dominant buying motives, and values. You confirm that need, and you offer a solution. It is unwise to offer a solution until you've established and confirmed a need. You then handle objections, you offer the close, and you deliver the congruent service. Finally, you ask for referrals. In this way you increase your productivity.

You can see hiring in much the same terms, because employees are, in a sense, buying the opportunity to work and earn income at your company. As the employer, you use a similar process to the one used in sales. You introduce yourself, create rapport with the potential employee, and establish their needs by determining their skills, track records, references, voids, and values. You confirm those histories and needs. You offer a service, which is a job description that fulfills the hiree's needs: it helps them get what they want, with an income that allows them to fill their voids. You also handle objections, which consists of what they see as *in* the way, not *on* the way. Then you deliver the service: you provide them with a job that matches their highest values. If you succeed, you will generate referrals: often you will see an inspired employee trying to get their friends to work there. All of these steps add to greater productivity.

The Evolution of Values

I'm sometimes asked why some values shift, some other values diminish or disappear altogether, and some seem to be enduring, even through an entire life.

Values evolve by two mechanisms, which are reflected in two hypotheses. One is called the *gradual hypothesis*, and the other is called the *punctuate hypothesis* or *cataclysmic hypothesis*.

The gradual hypothesis says that as we're going through life, when we encounter whatever's most meaningful to us, we tend to accelerate; we want to go further towards it. Conversely, we tend to withdraw from whatever challenges our values. In short, we tweak and remodel our hierarchy of values slowly but surely to adapt to an ever-changing environment. The punctuate hypothesis has to do with cataclysmic events, which can make us accelerate our pursuit of our value or stop it completely.

I'll give you an example. At one point, a lady attended my Breakthrough Experience seminar in Cape Town, South Africa. One day at noon, she had a car accident in which all of her four children died, although she survived. That morning, this woman was a mother; that afternoon, she was not. That's a cataclysmic event, so her values shifted. I worked with her until late into the evening, and when we finished, I helped dissolve her prolonged grief and transform her perception of the event in such a manner that she was in a state of gratitude for the transformation. This new perspective liberated her from her grief and allowed her to regain a new level of productivity and fulfillment.

In my case, I was born with my left arm and leg turned in. My arm and leg were put into clunky braces, which I had to wear up to age four. I begged my dad, "Please let me out of the restrictive braces. I promise to keep my arm and leg straight." When he let me out of the braces, all I wanted to do was run. I felt as if I had repressed all my running while watching other children run. Soon I began to run to school, run between classes, run outdoors—run everywhere. I would show my father how I could keep my arm and leg straight.

Because of that experience, I went into baseball, and I was exceptional; I was a top pitcher in baseball until age thirteen. At that point, my parents moved from Houston, where baseball was big, to Richmond, Texas, a small town where I was thirteen miles away from anybody that could play ball; we were a mile away from the nearest neighbor. Eventually, I managed to find a team to play baseball with, but as I've mentioned, we lived in a poor area, with gangs. If I struck out a player, later I would be beaten, sliced, or stabbed.

Still, I knew I wanted to be in sports, because I wasn't passing in school and had already dropped out. I pursued my second sport, surfing, because nobody was going to hit me with chains or stab me with knives out in the water. I could rely on myself in nature, and I also knew I had developed a relatively decent ability to maintain balance once I was freed from my braces. So I went into surfing, and I excelled. I went on to hitchhike to California and Mexico at age fourteen and eventually flew to Hawaii at fifteen, where I rode big waves on the north shore of Oahu.

But at age seventeen, I got strychnine poisoning and nearly died: I was unconscious for three and a half days. A lady found me in my tent, helped me recover, and took me to the health food store. That's where I saw a flyer to meet an inspired teacher whose name was Paul C. Bragg. In one hour, with one message, he inspired me to believe that I could overcome my learning and speaking challenges and begin to read and speak. Until I met him that night, I did not believe I could ever read and speak effectively. I discovered that maybe, just maybe, I might be able to awaken my intelligence. That was a huge void that has driven me ever since.

Those cataclysmic events changed my life. We grow through evolutionary leaps like that; the cataclysmic challenges make us take the biggest jumps. The biggest, most cataclysmic changes in your life are trying to get you to fulfill your greatest void and value-based mission, which is the key to great productivity.

Sharpening Your Vision

I'm also often asked, what action steps are required to sharpen and define your vision and attain maximum evolvement and growth?

Throughout your life, you will necessarily have and require both supporters and challengers. Maximum growth and development as well as maximum productivity occur at the border of support and challenge. That's why most companies will have within and around them both supporters and challengers, cooperators and competitors.

It's essential. It keeps growth, innovation, and productivity going and growing.

Whenever somebody supports your values, you tend to put them up on a pedestal. Whenever somebody challenges your values, you tend to put them in a pit. You open up to anyone who supports your values. You close down to anybody who challenges your values. This you admire; that you despise.

If you're your true self, you live according to your own hierarchy of values, and you base your decisions on that. But when you inject someone else's values into your life, you minimize and subordinate yourself in regard to that individual. You attempt to be other than who you are, and your vision becomes clouded. A clouded vision results from the injection of values of people you admire, which distract you from being present with your own highest value.

That's why the celebrated consultant W. Edwards Demming indirectly said that a manager cannot manage anyone that they are infatuated with or resent. If you are infatuated, you can't get them out of your mind. That will distract you from being present; it will cloud your vision and message and make you hesitate and lose your focus. The same is true of whomever you resent or despise. Whatever you are excessively attracted to or repelled from runs you.

Most managers, out of ignorance, reflect the Peter principle: they rise to their level of incompetence. Incompetence emerges once you become infatuated or resentful about what you attempt to manage. If a manager becomes infatuated with a highly productive employee, they can unwisely begin to think that everybody should be a high performer like this individual. By the law of contrast, the manager can also begin to resent the underperformer, which ends up breeding further resentment and disrupting the management environment of the business.

This kind of infatuation can occur with employees on the inside or with other companies on the outside. I had the opportunity in Australia to work with a leading bank CEO. A number of years ago, all the banks throughout Australia were having a rough time, but this particular CEO's bank started to lose market share—especially in regard to its primary competitor.

At first, the CEO thought it was a temporary glitch. As his bank's market share continued to drop, he became anxious. He started to think that the CEO of his competitor might have some knowledge and was using a strategy that he needed to follow, even though months earlier, while he was riding high, he was condemning the other bank's tactics. Now he was thinking he would have to incorporate a few of those tactics to save his own bank from market turmoil.

That created confusion inside him. He was now afraid of being himself in front of the people he worked with. He was afraid because he was trying to go against what he had just been preaching. He was wondering, "How do I rapidly change my bank's culture?" But you don't turn around a ship that size overnight. He was in turmoil; he wasn't sleeping. Most CEOs face this challenge during certain portions of the business market cycle. No CEO keeps rising and rising without hitting these limits of competence and experiencing uncertainties and volatilities.

I used the Demartini Method with this CEO. The Demartini Method, which I will explore in the next chapter, involves owning the traits of the people you admire to level the perceptual playing field so you don't have to be somebody you're not. You own the traits that you see in your competitor, because each of the many traits, "good" and "bad," lie somewhere within each of us.

As soon as the CEO completed this methodology, he ceased being infatuated with his competitor and stopped questioning his own initiatives. He realized that he had the same behaviors, and equally valuable strategies, as the other CEO, just in different forms. He honored the form that he himself displayed or demonstrated, which was congruent with his original vision, and he communicated more clearly and with renewed vigor the steps he was going to take to turn his company around.

At this time there was an overall movement against all the banks, but after this CEO did this process, he rode through that adverse weather more patiently and confidently. He had a clearer vision, because his vision had been cloudy when he temporarily subordinated himself. This occurs at any level of management, but it has the biggest impact at the top.

This particular CEO was savvy enough to act quickly; it entailed going back to his basic vision of customer service. He didn't have to change anything other than adding emphasis to what had been previously encouraged. If you're doing what has been proved to work—communicating to people's highest values—you get market share back. The key is not to let the outer perturbations distract your true inner and authentic mission.

In short, a clouded mind and vision result from infatuation with or resentment toward those you admire or despise, either within or outside the company. These emotional distractions reduce overall productivity, particularly when they create a chain reaction down through the ranks.

Can Government Change?

I'm often asked about educating those in government. Could there be a change in a country's economy if those in government were shown a different perspective on life?

Yes. In fact, if political leaders are not involved in continually educating and developing themselves, they're not going to understand how to grow a sustainable nation. True and caring long-term visionary leaders educate and encourage their people (though not to the point where everybody's an intellectual and nobody wants to work at the bottom). People who become more educated also have a higher probability of being congruent with their highest values. Moreover, if you educate the people in larger numbers, in democratic nations they're the voters, so they will have a different set of priorities or values, and their demands will change. As a result, the leaders will change in their leadership approaches as well.

Ideally, that's what the mass media was initially designed for—providing guidance and direction—although today it's mainly geared towards subjectively biased sensationalism. But again, many people want immediate gratification, because they're unfulfilled in their jobs and lives.

In any case, if you inspire people to live according to their highest values, you change the course of business, economics, and history. Your business will change the course of history if you apply even a portion of the productivity enhancing ideas I am presenting in this book.

Chapter 7
Obstacles

U p to this point, we've explored some of the many keys to productivity. Simply put, the way to accomplish twice as much in half the time is to focus on your highest values, be more inspired and authentic by delegating tasks that are related to lower values, say no to tasks that are irrelevant to your purpose, and compare your actions to your own highest values, not to those of others you admire or despise.

Now it's time to turn to the obstacles that may be keeping you from carrying out these aims.

Overcoming Regrets

Like many people, you may catch yourself thinking, "I wish I had done this," "I shouldn't have done that," or "I really messed up here." You may even believe that you've somehow "sabotaged" or limited yourself and carry feelings of regret as a result.

I'm a firm believer that anything you can't say thank you for is baggage, and anything you can say thank you for is fuel.

Whenever you feel regret, ashamed, or guilty about something you've done, it likely means that you have expected yourself to do something different from what you did—some moral ideal to which you compared your action. You probably also assumed that whatever you did had more drawbacks than benefits, either to yourself or another individual.

Every event has two sides. In fact, everything that's ever happened in your life has both an upside and a downside simultaneously. If you focus on the downside without looking for an upside, you'll likely feel regret or resentful.

It is wiser to bring your conscious awareness into full awareness, where you can simultaneously see both sides.

Human beings often display an amygdala-based subjective bias: an assumption that their life is more one-sided than it really is. This belief results in seeing a positive without a negative or a negative without a positive—a false positive and a false negative. This subjectively biased interpretation of your reality has a place when you are experiencing an emergency or in survival mode—like when an animal is trying to capture its supportive prey and avoid its challenging predator—but it can be unproductive when you persistently want to thrive and excel.

A false positive is when you see something that's not there, and a false negative is when you don't see something that *is* there.

When you don't live congruently with your highest priority, your blood, glucose, and oxygen flow into the subcortical region of your brain, including your amygdala. Imbalanced perceptions, which activate the amygdala, give rise to subjective bias and misinterpretation, which are the source of many regrets and resentments in life.

Once you balance your perceptions, you are able to dissolve the regrets. Note: not "live with" or "come to terms with" your regrets, but *dissolve* your regrets.

I'm a firm believer that whatever you've done in life is ultimately "on the way" and not "in the way," unless you choose to see it that way. That's your own perception, or misperception.

You have control of your perceptions, decisions, and actions.

If you choose to perceive an event as a nightmare, it can stay a nightmare. However, if you find out how whatever you've done or what you perceive has been done to you has served others or yourself equally, you become liberated. The Taoists understand that there is some yin inside the yang and some yang in side the yin. So too we can recognize that within the so-called terrible is some terrific and within the so-called terrific is some terrible. Perceiving one-sidedness is more distracting and less productive than perceiving both-sidedness (except during these emergencies).

In the next chapter, I will explore the Demartini Method, which helps you balance your perceptions and dissolve emotions such as rage, guilt, shame, anger, and regret. One application of this method involves going to a moment where and when you perceive yourself displaying or demonstrating some specific behavior that you dislike in yourself or someone else or that you perceived has caused pain, loss, regret, or resentment to you or somebody else.

In other words, you take the time to itemize exactly who you perceive was supposedly affected by it.

The next step may surprise you, because it involves asking the question: how did this same trait or action *serve* them or me? If you choose not to look for the upside, you'll probably live with unnecessary regret or resentment in your life.

I often encourage people not to give up too easily when asking themselves this question, because it may seem foreign and challenging if you have become accustomed to projecting or playing the victim in your life. It is wise to hold yourself accountable to balancing out the equation. In this way, you will be able to more masterfully govern and balance your perceptions and become neutral and objective instead of reactive and subjective. This gives rise to a more resourceful and productive state.

When you're perceiving an event or situation as one-sided, you tend to see more drawbacks than benefits, or benefits than drawbacks. By not seeing the upsides, you unnecessarily trap others or yourself in self-judgment and self-deprecation, because you never asked the questions: What were the upsides? What were the benefits? How did this serve me or them?

As you become conscious of the benefits, you will experience your levels of resentment or regret going down.

What if some action you did was perceived to have affected someone else, and you believe it caused them more pain than pleasure, more loss than gain, more negatives than positives?

In these instances, my reply is, take the time to stop and look, because no event has only one side. There's no event that doesn't have upsides to what you may currently perceive as only downsides. I have seen hundreds of examples where people have dissolved and balanced their perceptions of ostensibly unthinkable events and liberated themselves from years of regret or resentment.

Some of these initial judgments are due to local social contracts and even moral hypocrisies that people have absorbed from those higher up the social ladder, to whom they have given power. Though useful at times in certain settings of society, these attitudes can trap people in moral paradoxes for life if they are not transcended.

One event that comes to mind is a gentleman who was kidnapped and ransomed for a huge sum of money, which in his perception "caused" a great deal of distress and emotion both for him and his family. He had been diagnosed with posttraumatic stress disorder and found it challenging to live each day with the anger, bitterness, and resentment that he felt were consuming him.

I asked him, "What was the benefit of what happened to you?" He was slightly taken aback and quickly responded that there was absolutely no benefit whatsoever. He asked how I could even think there could be a benefit to what he and his family had been through.

My response, again, appeared to surprise him. I replied that when you have an absolute, moral, hypocritical view about life that's black-and-white without any gray, you tend to not be adaptable or resilient. Resilience has a lot to do with the ability to see both sides of a situation at the same time.

You fear the loss of what you are highly infatuated with. You fear the gain of what you are highly resentful of. When you are more objective and neutral, your fears subside.

I asked this man to hold himself accountable to looking for the benefits. After a while, he responded that he had been spending far more time with his family since the event. He went on thinking for a while and then told me about another benefit: he had restructured and prioritized his work life so he could delegate more in order to spend more time doing what he loved and head home at a more reasonable hour. He added that his wife too had felt inspired to go after what she truly wanted in life, because she had realized how quickly life can change.

After continuing the process and stacking up even more benefits, this man realized that the eventuality he had perceived as being so terrible wasn't so terrible after all.

We were able to dissolve his resentment towards what had happened, the guilt and shame he carried as a result of his perception that he had not adequately protected his family more, and the many emotions that had been weighing him down.

I am certain that there's no reason for you to carry unnecessary burdensome emotions. Polarized emotions are simply due to an incomplete awareness, or imbalanced ratios of perception.

Most people assume that they need to recover from and learn to live with the repercussions of a so-called traumatic event. I challenge that model and believe it to be antiquated. I think an event has occurred that you have consciously or unconsciously *chosen* to perceive as being traumatic.

It's not the event; it's your perception of it.

Great philosophers have been saying this for centuries, but many people prefer to run a story about how they are victims. As a result, they often create a false attribution bias about what other people "did to them" or what they "did to other people." They seem to be more comfortable in a moral, hypocritical world of one-sidedness instead of a world where both sides simultaneously and inseparably exist.

If you expect yourself to always be nice, never mean; kind, never cruel; generous, never stingy; always giving, never taking—in other words, to only be one-sided, you have created a complete moral fantasy and an unrealistic expectation for yourself. Whenever you don't match up to those unrealistic expectations, you're likely to experience regret and shame and feel that you're letting yourself or others down.

Realistic expectations, combined with asking quality questions, can dissolve such self-imposed regret.

I remember a man who was brought to my Breakthrough Experience in what can only be described as a catatonic state. He just sat and stared without speaking or interacting. I soon learned that he had been named and shamed for a massive explosion at the Phillips 66 refinery in the Pasadena, Texas, area that had killed twenty-three people and injured over 300. In brief, he was assumed responsible for an aged and faulty part called the valve O-ring. When it leaked, dehydrated, and oxidized, the explosion resulted. At that time, very little could have been done to prevent it, but the company needed a scapegoat, and he was it.

He just couldn't handle the international publicity, together with the fact that he blamed himself. This resulted in his catatonic state, which his psychiatrist or medical professional had not been able to break through.

When the time was right during the seminar and while everyone was working their way through an individual self-reflecting process, I knelt down in front of him and tried to make eye contact with him. It was as if I wasn't even there.

So I began listing the benefits and subsequent technological developments that had taken place with the O-ring and safety standards and explosion prevention as a result of the explosion.

Industry's pursuit of safe process design and operation started long before that explosion, which occurred on October 23, 1989. At that time, process safety management (PSM) was much different from what it is today. For example, there were no process safety engineers in industrial divisions. Nor were any process safety coordinators directing site compliance activities according to PSM principles. In fact, the federal Occupational Safety and Health Administration's PSM standard, which revolutionized the uniform application of safe process design and operating practices, was not published until almost three years later. Significant progress from these developments has made industry safer. Through these advancements, countless catastrophic process releases have been prevented, and many lives saved.

I told this man about new systems that had been put into place, enforced periodic replacements of the O-ring to ensure they didn't become oxidized, and the many upgrades to safety protocols and procedures that had been implemented.

I told him how if it weren't for that event, further lives could have been lost on an even greater scale, and that the overall death rate from injuries and explosions had since dropped, so while lives had indeed been lost, lives had also been saved as a result.

I continued listing even more benefits until we got to seventy-nine in total, and then I got the whole seminar group involved to stack up as many more as we could come up with. The more we wrote down, the more he cried. He finally had some relief from the weight of the shame, self-blame, and regret he had been carrying since the accident. I later learned that he had returned to work within weeks of his time at the Breakthrough Experience.

Every event is neutral until somebody with a subjective bias labels it as good or bad. As John Milton wrote, "The mind is its own place, and in itself / Can make a heaven of hell, a hell of heaven." It's about perception. I've been teaching people this process for nearly four decades, helping them take and cognitively reappraise their perceptions. I have yet to find anything they thought was terrible that we couldn't find the terrific in, or anything they thought was terrific that we couldn't find the terrible in. In fact, each event is neither until someone with a narrow view or subjectively biased mind makes it so.

Bronnie Ware, the Australian author of a beautiful book entitled *The Top Five Regrets of Dying*, wrote about the most frequent regrets people speak about at the end of their life. These include having the courage to be more true to themselves, not working so hard, expressing their feelings more, staying in touch with their friends, and giving themselves permission to be fulfilled.

I believe that regrets are unnecessary if you ask the right questions, because the quality of your life is based on the quality of the questions you ask. You can become conscious of upsides of which you may have been unconscious, and you can stack up the benefits; you can dissolve your regret or resentment and bring balance to your perceptions. Regrets and resentments are simply imbalanced perspectives, and as I mentioned before, you have full control over your perceptions if you ask quality questions to help you balance them. By balancing your perceptions, your mind becomes clear and less distracted, which enhances your creativity and productivity.

You're Never Too Old

You may feel that it's too late to make major changes in life, whether you're sixty-five or twenty-five.

A number of years ago, I had the opportunity to have a few meetings with the English-American theoretical physicist and mathematician Freeman Dyson. He was undoubtedly one of the brightest men I have ever met.

Until his death in 2020 at the age of ninety-seven, he was still researching and doing presentations at the Institute for Advanced Study at Princeton. There was no idea in his mind, or the minds of others, that he was too old to continue to live an extraordinary life—one of continued learning.

I have another friend, Bill Pollock, who runs Drake International, a massive corporation that he founded in 1951, while in his nineties. One night at a French restaurant in Sydney, Australia, he told me that the day he began the company was the last day he ever worked, because since then, he has gotten out of bed every morning to do what he loves to do. At an age that many may perceive as being "too old," he continues to be a vital and inspiring individual.

Then there's Mike Fremont, a marathon runner and holder of four world records who continues to lace up at the age of 100 years old.

Another example is Paul Biya, the president of Cameroon, who is eighty-nine, not to mention the late Queen Elizabeth II of the United Kingdom, who continued to run a major global enterprise until her passing at the age of ninety-seven.

The Dalia Lama is eighty-seven. Martha Stewart began the Home Shoppers Network at fifty. Bernie Marcus opened Home Depot when he was fifty. Colonel Lyman Sanders was in his sixties when he founded Kentucky Fried Chicken, and the founders of McDonalds were reportedly in their fifties. Ariana Huffington began the Huffington Post website when she was fifty-five. Some of my greatest achievements took place in my fifties and into my sixties.

Regardless of your age, it's never too late, and you're never too old. It's also never too early, and you're never too young. Age doesn't really matter: your perception, decisions, and actions are what matters. You can be ever more productive at any age any time, any place. It has a lot to do with your attitude.

As William James stated: "The greatest revolution in my generation was the discovery that human beings, by changing their inner attitudes of mind, can alter the outer aspects of their lives."

If you perceive that you may be too old, too out of touch, too young, or too inexperienced to start a new enterprise or move into a new position, it is wise to ask yourself:

How specifically is my current age giving me more advantage than disadvantage? What are the upsides and the advantages I have for being my age?

If you ask that question, and hold yourself accountable to repeatedly answer it twenty or more times, you might just surprise yourself with what you discover. You might suddenly find out that your age is to your advantage.

I've hired people in their teens and twenties who are enthusiastic, filled with ideas, and brimming with energy. I've also hired people in their sixties who were mature, diligent, experienced, and reliable. It's not about your chronological age as much as your psychological age. So how are you going to turn your age into your opportunity? The more congruent you are with living according to your highest values, the more vitality, creativity, and productivity you will display or demonstrate, regardless of age.

Fear as a Friend

If, like many other people I've worked with over the past four decades, you cite fear as your number one concern and hindrance, it is wise to remember that fear is also a friend.

Fear can be defined as the assumption that you're about to experience more negatives than positives, more losses than gains, and more disadvantages than advantages from whatever may happen to you in the future. You are anticipating an eventuality that will have more drawbacks than benefits.

Like everything else you will experience in your life, fear is accompanied by its opposite: a fantasy of having more advantages than disadvantages.

Think of a magnet: the one end or pole is labeled positive and the other end or pole is labeled negative.

The positive, philic pole represents the assumption that you're about to have more positives than negatives in the future. You may have philia or fantasy about the future or become infatuated with the future.

The negative, phobic pole represents the assumption that you're about to have more negatives than positives or more drawbacks than benefits in the future.

Philic fantasies and phobic fears are pairs of opposites. And, just like the positive and negative poles of a magnet, they both occur simultaneously.

You can't have one without the other.

Let's look at an example: meeting somebody and becoming infatuated with them. In this instance, you have a fantasy or philia about a future with them where you perceive there will be more positives than negatives. Simultaneously, you will consciously or unconsciously experience the opposite feelings, because you will also experience the phobic fear of losing that individual. You fear the loss of that which you become infatuated with.

Let's flip this situation on its head: you are resentful of someone. For example, you may resent someone you work with and fantasize escaping from them so you don't need to deal with them anymore. At the same time, you fear the gain of having to see more of them each day.

In other words, you fear the loss of that which you seek and are infatuated with.

You also fantasize about escaping a situation you fear or perceive to have more drawbacks than benefits.

You won't have one without the other. There's no philia without phobia, because you're going to fear the loss of what you desire, and there's no phobia without philia, because you're going to desire to escape what you dislike.

Philias and phobias come in pairs.

Whenever you have an imbalanced perspective that immobilizes you or hypermobilizes you, it is wise to do the work to balance your perceptions. This will enable you to be balanced, objective, neutral, aware of both the upsides and the downsides simultaneously, and able to mitigate risk and make proactive instead of reactive decisions. This clearer state of mind is a more productive state than when you are distracted by infatuations and resentments, or philias and phobias, which occupy space and time in your mind.

Let me elaborate on this point, because it underpins much of what I teach.

Like every individual, you have a set of priorities. Whenever your actions in life are congruent with your highest value or priority, you are more objective and reasonable and less polarized by emotions. You are therefore less likely to fear the loss of what you're seeking or the gain of what you're avoiding. You're also more likely to be more resilient, adaptable, and present and to take spontaneously inspired action to accomplish your goals.

However, when you allow yourself to pursue your lower values, you will function from the more emotionally reactive subcortical part of the brain. This area of the brain wants to avoid pain and seek pleasure, so it results in more subjectively biased and polarized perceptions and emotions. When you seek something, you fear its loss, and when you try to avoid something, you fear its gain. This survival mentality makes you more likely to become immobilized by phobias and hypermobilized by fantasies.

If, for example, you have self-limiting and polarized perceptions about your age—say that it may be too late for extraordinary achievements—you tend to be more vulnerable about this subject instead of being objective and balanced, able to see both the positives and negatives, upsides and downsides.

There is a series of fears that people tend to have that stem from such imbalanced perspectives.

1. The fear of not knowing enough, of not being smart enough.
2. The fear of not achieving or fear of failing.
3. The fear of losing money or not making money.
4. The fear of losing loved ones or the respect of loved ones.
5. The fear of rejection or not fitting into the group.
6. The fear of ill health, death, disease, or loss of vitality or beauty.
7. Fears of breaking the morals and ethics of some spiritual authority or moral hypocrisy that you've indoctrinated yourself with.

These fears are the result of seeking their corresponding fantasies.

If you have a fantasy of being successful, you likely also have a fear of failure.

If you have a fantasy of knowing something, you likely also have the fear of not knowing something or forgetting.

In other words, philias and phobias are pairs of opposites. They are compounded symptoms accentuated in your mind when you are not living congruently with your highest values.

When you live congruently, you're far more likely to be resilient, adaptable, neutral, and objective, with fewer phobias, fantasies, and distractions. You'll also be more likely to set real goals in real time frames and take intrinsic, inspired, and spontaneous actions to achieve. In this state, you are the most productive.

This state of mind also enables you to be fully present. In this state, you're far less likely to be comparing yourself to the past or future and more likely to simply take action in the present.

When you're not living congruently with your highest values, you are more likely to misinterpret the world you see, exaggerate the positives and the negatives, fear loss or gain, and become immobilized or hypermobilized. The likely outcome is uncertainty and unproductive distraction. When you are uncertain, you often begin making excuses and hold yourself back from achieving.

The Demartini Method, which I will explore in the next chapter, will enable you to break free of the fears and resistances that keep you from living congruently with your own highest values.

The Value of Anger

You can probably recall a number of times in your life when you've experienced deep anger and rage. You may not yet understand the profound purpose of anger: why it's there, where it originates, and the effect it may have on your physiology if you do not harness what it has to teach you.

We've already seen in some detail that productivity has to do, first and foremost, with living in accordance with your own unique highest values. As you go down your hierarchy of values, your values tend to be more extrinsic and require more outside motivation, reminders, or incentives to get you to act, which is less efficient, effective, and productive in life.

When you expect yourself to live outside your own highest values, you're likely to defeat yourself. When you expect yourself to live outside what you value most, you're likely to become self-deprecatory and angry at yourself.

The same applies to other people. When you expect anyone to live outside their unique set of highest values, they're likely to let you down. An individual invariably perceives, decides, and acts based on what they value most. Every decision they make is based on what they believe will give them the greatest advantage over disadvantage to their highest values at any moment. Whenever you expect a human being to live outside what they value most, you're likely to be let down, because they're much less likely to do what you expect them to do.

They're not wrong for being who they are, but you may be unwise in expecting them to be what they're not inspired to be, because you have not considered their true individual hierarchy of values. Because their identity revolves around their highest values—that's who they intrinsically are—you can rely on them to make decisions that tend to align with their own higher values, not yours and not the social idealisms you may have expected and projected onto them.

When you expect another human being to live in your values or outside their own, you'll tend to experience feelings of anger and aggression, feel betrayed and want to falsely attribute blame to them, criticize them, and challenge them back. You may feel depressed and despairing. You may want to exit and escape, feel frustrated and futile, grouchy and grieving, hate them and hurt them, and be irritable and irrational around them—because you're expecting them to live outside what they value most.

Anger is due to unmet expectation. If your expectations are unrealistic, you're most likely to be angry, because others aren't meeting them. Furthermore, whenever you expect yourself or others to be one-sided, you're likely to be angry—either at them or at yourself.

This leads us to an apparently surprising conclusion: your anger towards others or yourself is a valuable feedback mechanism to let you know that you have unrealistic expectations.

Blaming somebody for not living up to your unrealistic expectations is delusional. You can reasonably expect a human being only to live according to their own highest values, not necessarily yours or those of someone else in society.

When you get angry, you also create physiological feedback. Your anger over your unmet expectations activates your sympathetic nervous system, which results in a fight-or-flight response. You'll tend to get angry, want to fight with them or avoid them, challenge them, and criticize them. Your blood sugar is likely to increase, your muscles get tense and tight, your digestive system shuts down, your testosterone goes up, and you get more aggressive. Your physiological symptoms are also providing valuable feedback to let you know you have an unrealistic expectation. In such a moment, it is wise to self-reflect a bit and look to see if you are not also self-righteously challenging this individual's highest values in some way without realizing it. You may need a bit of humbling to take you off the pedestal and back down to your own state of authenticity.

I believe that anger is not necessarily bad and, like fear, can be your friend. Every one of your behaviors serves some purpose. It's simply feedback telling you that you have unrealistic expectations. If anger did not somehow serve, it would have gone extinct.

Your anger is under your governance.

It's not what happens to you out there, but what you perceive and expect. If you expect an outcome that's not realistic, you're likely to be angry. This less resourceful state leaves you being less productive.

As such, I don't go by what people say, but by their hierarchy of values. Sometimes people don't want to upset you, so they'll tell you what you want to hear. You'll then expect them to act accordingly and feel angry and betrayed when they don't.

Although the majority of people may have every intention initially of living up to their word, they may have unexpected situations or greater opportunities that arise later, and they will pursue those.

If someone acts in a different way than they said they would, instead of judging them or being harsh on them, find out what changed their decision. What came along that was so much more important to them that it overrode what was important to you? Ideally, they will inform you when they have changed their plans, but they may not do that if they feel you might use guilt trips or emotional blackmail to get them to do what they initially agreed on.

It may also be wise to reflect on where and when you have made the same change of plans on someone else. Projecting moral ideals and shoulds onto people will backfire.

People live according to their own set of values, not necessarily according to some form of collective idealism that you think they are supposed to live by.

Knowing your unique hierarchy of values, or highest priorities, and those you spend most of your time with, is the most important place to start if you would love to break through from a life of anger and reaction to a life of mastery and action.

Chapter 8

The Demartini Method

To begin, let me explain what the Demartini Method is. It is a systematic series of concise mental questions to help you neutralize and transform your disempowering, polarized emotional feelings, which can weigh you down, into more transcendent and integrated feelings of presence, certainty, inspiration, enthusiasm, gratitude, and love, which can lighten you up.

The Demartini Method is a cognitive, cortical, executive function development exercise. It is used to return your brain from a subcortical, emergency, survival response to a more fulfilling cortical, executive, thrival response. It is the culmination of more than five decades of research and studies in disciplines, including physics, philosophy, theology, metaphysics, psychology, astronomy, mathematics, neurology, and physiology.

It's a specific inquiring process that involves balancing your perceptions (similar to balancing mathematical or chemical equations) through a continuous action of questioning, answering, thinking and writing (or typing), which will lead you from lower, inner, and narrower to higher, outer, and broader brain functioning.

To begin with, each of your positively or negatively polarized emotions is a by-product of your imbalanced *ratio of perceptions*.

When you perceive that an event or situation has more benefits than drawbacks, you label it as *supportive or beneficial*. Here you are conscious of the upsides and unconscious of the downsides.

When you perceive that an event or situation has more drawbacks than benefits, you label it as challenging or detrimental. Here you are conscious of the downsides and unconscious of the upsides.

Most people act as if they have no power over their perceptions: they believe that a given situation is either supportive and beneficial or challenging and detrimental. They assign false attribution biases and causalities to how they feel, and they give credit or blame to outside circumstances instead of realizing that it is more about their own evaluative perceptions.

But you have the power to transform how you perceive an event by asking and accountably answering quality questions that bring balance back to your awareness. This means that you simultaneously see the up of the down and the down of the up. You see life in a more balanced manner and as "on the way" instead of "in the way." This manner is more productive than the imbalanced manner that disempowers and distracts.

When you bring your mathematical equation of perception into balance, your blood, glucose, and oxygen flow more into the prefrontal cortex or executive center of your forebrain. This area of your brain helps you become more objective and self-governed. This is known as the center of System 2 thinking, where you think before you emotionally feel and react. This is a more productive approach (except under extreme, life-threatening, emergency survival situations, which are generally rare).

By contrast, System 1 thinking is governed by the reactive amygdala or subcortical lower brain. It thinks fast and renders you reactive to the outer world instead of acting upon the world. In this state, you are more emotionally volatile, irrational, and likely to feel at the mercy of outer circumstances.

When you are operating in the brain area of your higher executive function, you open up your foresight. With that, you give birth to a clarity of vision and mission and you see strategically how to achieve it. When you learn the art of governing your mind, or developing your self-governing executive center, you become the captain of your ship, the master of your destiny, a visionary, and an inspired leader—an individual of authenticity and influence.

Demartinian Psychology

The Demartini Method incorporates the insights of Demartinian psychology, which integrates some of the strengths of many previously developed psychological methods, including behavioral, transpersonal, and cognitive psychologies.

It offers new practical, concise, and insightful questions to help you integrate conscious and unconscious portions of your awareness to help you, or the individual that you are facilitating the method with, to become more mindfully conscious. Demartinian psychology is about transcending the traditional victim model and awakening to an accountable, inner-directed, and self-reflective journey of transformation to empowerment.

Mind mastery is life mastery.

You've read enough now to understand some of the background to Demartinian psychology: It's focused on maximizing the development of the self-governing executive center of the brain (the prefrontal cortex) in order to override the less governed, more reactive subcortical regions of your brain. Developing your prefrontal cortex, the source of your self-governing executive function, is essential for mastering your life. The executive center is your true source of achievement power. It's the source of your authenticity, objectivity, resilience, higher brain reflection, strategic thinking, foresight, vision, mission and purpose. It is also the key area that lets you maximize your greatest productivity.

Demartinian psychology includes the use of fifty-eight executive function development exercises that form the principal methodology in the Demartini Method. It also incorporates human value–based strategies to help you, your clients, and your loved ones live more deeply meaningful and fulfilling lives. It's for individuals who are ready to take accountability for their perceptions, decisions, and actions and thereby unlock the door to mastering and fulfilling their lives.

The Tool with 1,000 Uses

Most psychological conditions originate from an imbalanced equation of perceptions. The Demartini Method is the science of restoring these perceptions back to balance. When you integrate your brain by balancing your perceptions, you function more from your forebrain, which means you are equipped to take command of your life again with foresight. This is called *governance* or *self-governance*.

You can use the Demartini Method to empower the seven major areas of life:

Spiritually. When you're in governance, you have equanimity, equity, and objectivity, and you're in a state of grace, inspiration, love and appreciation—true spiritual expression. This method:

- Awakens your mind to an underlying hidden order and greater intelligence found in nature.
- Opens your mind to greater wisdom and truth.
- Opens your heart to greater love and appreciation.

Mentally. By balancing the mathematical equation of perception, you balance your mind, and you rise up from the subcortical region of your brain to your more advanced prefrontal cortex, where you're more resilient, adaptable, and objective. This method:

- Organizes your ideas and thoughts, bringing order out of chaos.
- Expands your mind and awakens your intuitive faculties.

- Clears away your emotionally charged memories and imaginings.
- Helps you develop more certainty and presence.

Vocationally. Low levels of self-governance affect overall productivity and results. High levels of self-governance initiate greater leadership and help you build more sustainable business models and strategies. The method:

- Adds more certainty and clarity to your career direction.
- Enables you to see the pros and cons of decisions in advance, with more objectivity.
- Inspires greater inner drive and autonomy.
- Increases wise action and decreases foolish reactions.
- Increases the probability of more sustainable fair exchanges in transactions.

Financially. If you're proud and elated, or shamed and depressed, you'll spend your money foolishly and erode your wealth. But more authentic self-governance:

- Helps you develop greater self-worth.
- Helps you more patiently build long-term wealth.
- Decreases your tendency to make excuses, which undermines wealth building.
- Moderates over- or underspending.
- Expands your time horizons and patience.

Family. Awareness in relationships helps you:

- Build accountable and reflective connection and true intimacy.

- Enhance dialogue more than alternating monologues in communication.
- Resolve conflict.
- Decrease blame.
- Add respect and understanding.

Socially. Self-governance gives you the ability to rise above paradoxes and attain the objectivity required for leadership, which:

- Generates leadership qualities.
- Helps you break through philias and phobias, infatuations and resentments, pride and shame.
- Adds clarity to your mission, vision, and message, or purposeful direction.
- Brings higher ordered understanding to world events.

Physically. Your emotions are perturbing your physiology, creating symptoms to try to get you back into authenticity and governance. This method:

- Clears emotionally charged perceptions and their illness producing muscular compressions and tensions.
- Dissolves distress and adds vitality.
- Calms emotions and relaxes muscles.
- Makes you feel lighter and helps you sleep more soundly.

The Process

The Demartini Method is not difficult, but it requires that you be present and thorough. It can be applied in many different contexts: to other people, to yourself, to qualities you either admire or detest. The process is essentially the same, because every behavioral trait you perceive in someone else is one you possess yourself, whether you know it or not. Furthermore, every behavioral trait has both a positive and a negative aspect associated with it: that is a fundamental conservation law of the universe.

As a result, the method works the same way no matter where you start—on some behavioral trait you either admire or despise.

The Demartini Method consists of a series of questions. Let's take the example of using it on someone other than yourself. When you are answering the questions, it is wise to think categorically in the seven areas of life—spiritual, mental, vocational, financial, familial, social, physical—or to think chronologically from the past to the present. You go through these steps:

1. Identify the most admired emotional charges. Write (in three to four words for each) the top three highest priority specific traits, actions, or inactions (TAIs) that you perceive this individual displaying or demonstrating that you like or admire most. Make sure they are not derived from hearsay from others. Also make sure that you can pinpoint exactly where and when you perceived them occurring, and in what context.

Exclude synthesized transcendental feelings (like *loving* or *inspired*); serial synonyms (like *nice* or *kind*); vague generalities or labels (*good person, saintly,* or *good father*);

and how you felt as a result of perceiving this individual displaying or demonstrating this specific TAI (such as *I felt proud* or *I felt smart*).

When you have finished: Are you now certain that you have listed the top three specific (TAIs) that you perceive this individual has displayed or demonstrated that you most like, admire, look up to, are infatuated with, or consider positive or attractive?

2. Confirm laws of reflection and transparency. Go to a specific moment where and when you perceived yourself displaying or demonstrating this same or similar TAI that you most liked or admired in the individual from step 1. Then write down, in an abbreviated and overlapping format, where, when, and to whom you perceived yourself displaying or demonstrating this TAI and who perceived you doing so. Do this until you can state with certainty that you own this TAI 100 percent as much as you have perceived it in the other individual, both quantitatively and qualitatively. Consider all seven areas of your life from past to present. Those who perceived you displaying or demonstrating this TAI could be you, the individual you displayed or demonstrated it to, or another perceiver.

When you have finished: Are you now certain that you perceive yourself displaying or demonstrating this same or similar specific TAI 100 percent to the same degree, quantitatively and qualitatively? Are you now certain that there are others that have perceived you displaying or demonstrating this TAI?

3. Dissolve other-infatuation and self-minimization.
Go to the specific moment where and when you perceived this individual displaying or demonstrating this specific TAI that you liked or admired most. Then write down, in an abbreviated and overlapping format, how this TAI from that moment until today was a *drawback* or *disservice* to you (or another individual and you) in your three highest values and seven areas of life. Include primary, secondary, and tertiary drawbacks. Exclude any self-minimizing answers. Be sure that you are writing down the drawbacks or disservices of this specific TAI and not those of your doing the opposite, or of not displaying or demonstrating this TAI.

When you have finished: Are you now certain that the specific TAI listed in step 1 was just as equally a drawback or disservice to you (or another individual and you) as it was a benefit or service? Is it now neither positive or negative?

4. Dissolve self-infatuation and pride. Go to the specific moment where and when you perceive yourself displaying or demonstrating the same or similar specific TAI that you most like or admire in this individual. Then write how this specific trait, action, or inaction that you perceive yourself displaying or demonstrating is, in that moment and until today, a drawback or disservice to those to whom you have displayed or demonstrated this TAI—or to those perceiving you. Exclude any other-minimizing answers. Include primary, secondary, and tertiary drawbacks or disservices. Make sure that you do not go too far and transform your pride into shame. Check in every three answers to make sure you have not gone past the neutral state. Apply this step to each moment listed in step 2 until each moment becomes neither positive nor negative.

When you have finished: Are you now certain that the specific TAI in this individual you listed in step 1 (and reflected and confirmed equally in yourself in step 2) was just as equally a drawback or disservice to the others to whom you have demonstrated them? Is each now neither positive or negative?

5. Dissolve exaggerated labels and enhance communication, resiliency, and immunity. Go to a specific moment where and when you perceived this individual displaying or demonstrating the specific TAI that you like or admire most. Whom did you perceive them displaying or demonstrating the specific TAI to? Then write down, in an abbreviated and overlapping format, where and when you perceive this individual at any time displaying or demonstrating the exact opposite TAI to the same individual or group to whom they displayed or demonstrated the original TAI, and who perceived it. Keep writing until you are certain that the *exact opposite* specific TAI equals the *original* specific TAI, quantitatively and qualitatively. Do this for each individual to whom you perceived them displaying this specific TAI.

When you have finished: Are you now certain that this individual has displayed or demonstrated the specific trait, action, or inaction and the exact opposite specific trait, action, or inaction (anti-TAI) equally to the same individuals (yourself, others, or a group) to the same degree, quantitatively and qualitatively? Are you now certain there are no more subjective "alls" or "nones" or "always" or "nevers" applied to the description of their TAIs?

6. Demonstrate synchronicity, entanglement, and hidden intelligent order. Go to a specific moment where and when you perceive this individual displaying or demonstrating the specific TAI that you like or admire most. Where are you? When are you? Get present in the specific moment. Whom is this individual displaying or demonstrating this TAI to? What specifically is the content and context? Write, in an abbreviated and overlapping format, the initials of those individuals who displayed or demonstrated the exact opposite TAI to the same individual or group at the exact same moment. Make sure they are quantitatively and qualitatively equal and opposite. Exhaust all moments until each of the entangled opposites are synchronized. The answers could be: one individual/many individuals, male/female, close/distant, self/other, virtual/real.

When you have finished: Are you now certain that either you or some other individual was simultaneously displaying or demonstrating the exact opposite TAI that you perceived this individual displaying or demonstrating, either to you or a specific other individual? This is in order to synchronously balance out that specific TAI you listed in step 1, both quantitatively and qualitatively.

7. Dissolve nightmares and the driving forces of fantasies and philias. Go to a specific moment where and when you perceive this individual displaying or demonstrating the specific TAI that you liked or admired most. Then write, in an abbreviated and overlapping format, the *benefits* or *services* to you and to the specific other individual or group you perceived the individual was displaying or demonstrating this TAI to if this individual were to have displayed or demonstrating the *exact opposite* TAI—that is, the way you had wished or hoped they had *not* done. Include primary, secondary, and tertiary benefits or services. Go to each moment you perceived this individual displaying or demonstrating this specific TAI, and repeat this step.

When you have finished: Are you now certain that if you perceived the individual in question displaying the exact opposite specific trait, action, or inaction (anti-TAI) to that listed in step 1 at that same moment, there would have been just as many benefits, positives, or services as drawbacks, negatives, or disservices, quantitatively and qualitatively?

These seven steps are meant to show you that each trait you admire in someone else has an equal and opposite number of drawbacks and disadvantages. Furthermore, you possess exactly the same trait, which, again, has an equal and opposite number of drawbacks and advantages.

Let's now proceed to the negative version of this process.

8. Identify the most despised emotional charges.

Write (in three to four words for each) the top three highest priority specific traits, actions, or inactions (TAIs) that you perceive this individual displaying or demonstrating that you *dislike* or *despise* most.

When you have finished: Are you now certain that you have listed the top three specific (TAIs) that you perceive this individual has displayed or demonstrated that you most dislike, despise, look down upon, are resentful to, or consider negative or repulsive?

9. Confirm laws of reflection and transparency. Go to a specific moment where and when you perceived yourself displaying or demonstrating this same or similar TAI that you most *disliked* or *despised* in the individual from step 8. Then write down, in an abbreviated and overlapping format, where, when, and to whom you perceived yourself displaying or demonstrating this TAI and who perceived you doing so. Do this until you can state with certainty that you own this TAI 100 percent as much as you have perceived it in the other individual, both quantitatively and qualitatively. Consider all seven areas of your life from past to present. Those who perceived you displaying or demonstrating this TAI could be you, the individual you displayed or demonstrated it to, or another perceiver.

When you have finished: Are you now certain that you perceive yourself displaying or demonstrating this same or similar specific TAI 100 percent to the same degree, quantitatively and qualitatively? Are you now certain that there are others that have perceived you displaying or demonstrating this TAI?

10. Dissolve other-resentment and self-exaggeration. Go to the specific moment where and when you perceived this individual displaying or demonstrating this specific

TAI that you dislike or despised most (as listed in step 8). Then write down, in an abbreviated and overlapping format, how this TAI from that moment until today was a *drawback* or *disservice* to you (or another individual and you) in your three highest values and seven areas of life. Include primary, secondary, and tertiary drawbacks. Exclude any self-minimizing answers. Be sure that you are writing down the drawbacks or disservices of this specific TAI and not those of you doing the opposite, or of not displaying or demonstrating this TAI.

When you have finished: Are you now certain that the specific TAI listed in step 8 was just as equally a benefit or service to you (or another individual and you) as it was a drawback or disservice? Is it now neither negative or positive?

11. Dissolve self-minimization and shame. Go to the specific moment where and when you perceive yourself displaying or demonstrating the same or similar specific TAI that you most dislike or despise in this individual. Then write how this specific trait, action, or inaction that you perceive yourself displaying or demonstrating is, in that moment and until today, a *benefit* or *service* to those to whom you have displayed or demonstrated this TAI—or to those perceiving you. Exclude any other-minimizing answers. Include primary, secondary, and tertiary benefits or services. Make sure that you do not go too far and transform your shame into pride. Apply this step to each moment listed in step 9 until each moment becomes neither negative nor positive.

When you have finished: Are you now certain that the specific TAI in this individual you listed in step 8 (and reflected and confirmed equally in yourself in step 9) was just as equally a benefit or service to the others to whom you have demonstrated them to? Is each now neither negative or positive?

12. Dissolve exaggerated labels and enhance communication, resilience, and immunity. Go to a specific moment where and when you perceive this individual displaying or demonstrating the specific TAI that you dislike or despise most. Whom did you perceive them displaying or demonstrating the specific TAI to? Then write down in an abbreviated and overlapping format where and when you perceived this individual at any time displaying or demonstrating the exact opposite TAI to the same individual or group to whom they displayed or demonstrated the original TAI, and who perceived it. Keep writing until you are certain that the exact opposite specific TAI equals the original specific TAI quantitatively and qualitatively. Do this for each individual to whom you perceived them displaying this specific TAI.

When you have finished: Are you now certain that this individual has displayed or demonstrated the specific trait, action, or inaction (TAI) and the exact opposite specific trait, action, or inaction (anti-TAI) equally to the same individuals (yourself, others, or a group) to the same degree, quantitatively and qualitatively? Are you now certain there are no more subjective "alls" or "nones" or "always" or "nevers" applied to the description of their TAIs?

13. Demonstrate synchronicity, entanglement, and hidden intelligent order. Go to a specific moment where and when you perceive this individual displaying or demonstrating the specific TAI that you disliked or despised most. Where are you? When are you? Get present in the specific moment. Whom is this individual displaying or demonstrating this TAI to? What specifically is the content and context? Write in an abbreviated and overlapping format the initial(s) of those individuals who displayed or demonstrated the exact opposite TAI to the same individual or group at the exact same moment. Make sure they are quantitatively and qualitatively equal and opposite. Exhaust all moments until each of the entangled opposites are synchronized: one individual/many individuals, male/female, close/distant, self/other, virtual/real.

When you have finished: Are you now certain that either you or some other individual was simultaneously displaying or demonstrating the exact opposite TAI that you perceived this individual displaying or demonstrating, either to you or a specific other individual? This is in order to synchronously balance out that specific TAI you listed in step 8, both quantitatively and qualitatively.

14. Dissolve fantasies and the driving forces of nightmares and phobias. Go to a specific moment where and when you perceive this individual displaying or demonstrating the specific TAI that you disliked or despised most. Then write in an abbreviated and overlapping format the *drawbacks* or *disservices* to you and to the specific other individual or group you perceived the individual was displaying or demonstrating this TAI to if this individual were to have displayed or demonstrated the *exact opposite* TAI—that is, the way you had wished or hoped they had done. Include primary, secondary, and tertiary drawbacks or disservices. Go to each moment you perceived this individual displaying or demonstrating this specific TAI.

When you have finished: Are you now certain that if you perceived this individual displaying the exact opposite specific trait, action, or inaction (anti-TAI) to that listed in step 8 at that same moment, there would have been just as many drawbacks, negatives, or disservices as benefits, positives, or services, quantitatively and qualitatively?

To summarize the steps:

1. Identify a trait, action, or inaction (TAI) that you admire in someone else.

2. Identify a series of moments where and when you yourself have demonstrated the same TAI.

3. Identify, at each moment the individual demonstrated the TAI, what the drawbacks or disservices to you were.

4. Identify where and when you demonstrated the same TAI and at that moment what were drawbacks or disservices to those to whom you demonstrated the TAI.

5. Identify where and when this individual demonstrated the opposite TAI (anti-TAI) to the one identified in step 1 to the same individual they demonstrated the original TAI to.

6. Identify where and when you perceive one or more individuals simultaneously demonstrating the anti-TAI to

the same individual that this individual demonstrated the trait to.

7. Identify the benefits to you if this individual would have demonstrated the opposite anti-TAI at the moment they demonstrated the TAI you admired.

Steps 8 through 14 correspond exactly, except that these TAIs are those you dislike or despise.

Upon completing these above steps, the identified distracting emotionally charged judgments listed previously will be dissolved, and a more ordered executive state of neutral objectivity will emerge. This will free up inefficiently applied energy and direct it toward greater, more meaningful and productive, higher-priority actions. Whenever you become distracted by personal or professional infatuations or resentments, or compensatory states of pride or shame, the Demartini Method can assist you in dissolving them and liberating you to become more efficient and productive.

Chapter 9

The Ripple Effect

U p to this point, we have discussed the advantages of focusing on your highest value to yourself as well as removing some of the obstacles to you realizing or fulfilling this value. Now let's turn to the effects of our actions in a broader context.

An Old Bum on the Street

I love to tell the story of an experience I had when I was fourteen. For me, it beautifully demonstrates the ripple effect that one moment in an individual's life can have on another.

I was hitchhiking from Houston to Los Angeles with a small duffel bag and my surfboard and arrived in El Paso, Texas, en route. At this time, El Paso was largely made up of cowboys and cowgirls who weren't overly fond of surfers, especially a long-haired hippie type.

I was walking through town when I was confronted by three cowboys around the age of twenty. They looked as if they were going to aggressively beat me up. I didn't know what to do, so I began to growl, bark, and act like a wild dog, which actually worked and made them back off.

I didn't realize it in the moment, but there was a gentleman leaning against a lamppost who witnessed what had just happened.

He approached me and said, "Sonny, that is the funniest dang thing I've ever seen somebody do. You took care of them cowpokes like a pro. Can I buy you a cup of coffee?"

I told him that I didn't drink coffee but would appreciate a Coca-Cola, so he took me to a malt shop a couple of streets down, where we sat on swivel stools and began talking.

Soon into the conversation, he asked me if I was a runaway. I responded that my parents had given me a ride to the freeway so that I could hitchhike to California to go surfing. We chatted for a while further, and he told me that he had something to teach me and asked me to walk with him.

I was a little hesitant, as it's not every day that a gentleman over sixty takes an interest in a fourteen-year-old surfer and offers to teach him something.

We ended up walking a few blocks down the road and into the downtown El Paso library. This gentleman (I still didn't know who he was) sat me down before going to the bookshelves to find some books he was looking for.

When he returned, he placed two books on the table in front of me.

"Sonny," he said, "there are two things I would love to teach you. You have to promise me that you will never forget what I am about to tell you."

"Yes sir," I stated.

"Number one is, don't ever judge a book by its cover, because the cover can fool you. You might look at me and perceive that I am some old guy who lives on the street, but I am one of the wealthiest men in the world. I have everything that money can buy—planes, businesses, homes, and companies—so don't let a cover fool you."

He then took my hand and placed it on top of the two books he had taken from the shelves, one by Plato and the other by Aristotle. "Young man," he said, "there are only two things that people can never take away from you in your life. They can never take away your love, and they can never take away your wisdom. They can take away your possessions, friends, family, and everything else you have, but they can never take away your love and wisdom. So lesson number two is to gain the wisdom of love and the love of wisdom. Learn how to read."

He made me promise him that I would never forget those two lessons. Then he put the books back on the shelf and showed me which direction to take to hitchhike on to California.

I later found out that he was Howard Hughes, the legendary billionaire who was finalizing a business deal in El Paso with El Paso Natural Gas company for a brewery.

I happened to be in the right place at the right time and met the right individual who said what I needed to hear. Although I didn't realize it at the time, my life changed that day.

Because of that man's ripple effect on my life, today I have cufflinks that say "love" and "wisdom." It's also how I sign off on my emails. Instead of saying "kind regards," I say, "love and wisdom." And all of my research, writing, and teaching today are dedicated to mastering and disseminating love and wisdom.

You may not initially or fully realize that chance experiences such as this can have a such a massive impact.

I doubt if Howard Hughes ever knew what happened to me and how that chance encounter would change my life.

A similar experience happened a few years later when I met a man by the name of Paul C. Bragg, another individual, whom I mentioned earlier. He too said something that changed the trajectory of my whole life: contrary to what I'd been previously told, he said that I was able to overcome my learning problems and learn how to read effectively. He told me to say to myself every single day for the rest of my life: *I am a genius and I apply my wisdom.* I have not missed a single day saying this to myself for over fifty years. It changed my path and mission for life, and it massively impacted my productivity and achievements.

My life today is largely the result of meeting Howard Hughes on a street at age fourteen and Paul Bragg at the age of seventeen.

Your Daily Impact

It is wise to pay close attention to the impact you may have on a day-to-day basis. Your impact and productivity may be greater than you think.

The ripple effect of your life might be greater than you initially imagine.

You may believe that you can only make a global impact by acting on a massive scale, but that's not always the case. You can make a massive difference by raising a child. You could make a massive difference by supporting local, owner-managed stores in your area. You could make a massive difference by giving someone a sandwich when they have nothing to eat. You can make a massive difference by saying something that changes another individual's life, as Howard Hughes changed mine.

You might be reaching and impacting millions of people without even knowing it. You might be changing decisions about what people do in their life. You may be the catalyst for someone's career choice, whom they end up marrying, or why they decide to master their destiny instead of remaining a victim of their history.

An exercise I like to share, and one that I encourage you to do, is to write down the ripple effects that you have in your life.

Look at all seven areas of your life—spiritual, mental, professional, financial, familial, social, and health-related—so you can begin to perceive the impact that you have.

1. Make a list of everything you might do in a day, week, or month. Itemize each task, and identify the direct or indirect impact it has on the people and world around you.

2. Creatively brainstorm the impact that you've had by your presence, the people you've touched, the lessons you've learned, the places you've gone, what you've said, and what you've done. Meditate on the impact that each of those acts may have had on your life and on the lives of people around you.

3. It is wise to look at all seven areas of your life and not stop until your mind is open-hearted and you are blown away by the impact you're making and have already made. It is also wise to keep going until you experience tears of inspiration and gratitude in your eyes about the impact of your very presence.

It may blow your mind to discover that what you do may be far more significant than first meets the eye. You may realize that you've been minimizing yourself.

As I often say, when you value yourself, so does the world. When you minimize yourself, so does the world.

Taking the time to do this exercise might reveal that the ripple effect of your life is greater than you imagined.

The moment you value yourself and realize you're making a greater difference than you have previously perceived, the way that you perceive yourself relative to the world changes. It doesn't grow arrogant, but it does become more confident. It doesn't exaggerate itself; instead, it is balanced by looking at the facts.

This is not about imagining delusory scenarios. It is about expanding your mind and opening your heart so you can become aware of the authentic impact you have and the resulting ripple effects. Once you begin to see this greater impact, which you already have, the more you will be inspired to serve and the greater and more productive actions you will begin to take.

Chapter 10

It's All Spiritual

Your spiritual perspective can impact your degree of productivity. Let's see how. Since the age of eighteen, I have been inspired to master all seven areas of my life— spiritual, mental, professional, financial, familial, social, and physical, but I only really began to dig much more deeply into spirituality, comparative religion, and philosophy in my early twenties.

My first step was to explore the many encyclopedias of world religions so I could find and make a list of every form of religion, mythology, mystery school cult, mythology, or esoteric group with a specific religious or spiritual understanding that professed to have 50,000 followers or more.

I read as much as I could get my hands on, visited a variety of synagogues, mosques, ashrams, temples, and churches, and met with locally or globally impacting yogis, gurus, mystics, imams, monks, lamas, priests, ministers, philosophical teachers, and more so I could document as many similarities or common threads and differences as I could.

Eventually, having explored around 3,000 different religions and cults, I came to a conclusion that may be quite shocking to some people:

It's all spiritual.

I also realized that in many cases, spirituality was and still is commonly associated with the deification of a plant or animal (zoomorphism), a human (anthropomorphism), a rock, mountain or whole planet (geomorphism), or a star (astromorphism). In fact, if you study the evolution of the concept of the gods, you'll see that they are mostly personifications of some forces or bodies of nature, such as the rain, wind, thunder, lightning, sun, planets, moon, plants, animals, or humans.

I also discovered that if you look at the entire evolution of religion from animism and shamanism to mysticism to metaphysics and philosophy, and eventually into science and abstract mathematics, you could see how it reflects the evolution of the human brain. All of it has been part of an innate spiritual or inspirational quest of human beings throughout the ages.

Everything—the galaxies, the stars, the planets, the earth, stones, plants, animals, and humans—has been worshiped and appreciated. Some older systems have become extinct along the way, and many deities that used to be worshiped have been transcended, having faded and become forgotten.

It was then that I realized that spirituality is an expression of the developing human brain. It has reflected and still reflects the various portions and functions within the human brain and/or mind.

I also realized that spirituality is not limited to any particular religion, deity, set of deities, languages, or locations. It is much broader.

I started looking at the roles of the amygdala and the prefrontal cortex of the brain in different religious understandings. I also spent time researching transmitters and regulators and different regions of the cortex in which, when you magnetically stimulate them, you can create religious experiences. I studied dissociative posttraumatic states, near-death experiences and ecstatic meditation brain correlations.

After fifty years of research, I came to define *spirituality* as *that which inspires and brings meaning and fulfillment to the individual.* And this can be as varied in form as the number of individuals on earth.

Some people are inspired by raising a beautiful family of children; that is their spiritual path. Others are inspired to run a successful business, that is their spiritual path. Still others are inspired by intellectual pursuits, and that is theirs. Some express their spirituality within organized religions. That is their spiritual path. Others are inspired by wealth and go on to create massive companies and build fortunes. That too is spiritual. Each of these is inspiring, but various other pursuits can also be perceived as unique forms of productivity.

I remember chatting with a lady who asked for my input on how she could navigate her relationship with her husband, whom she perceived as not being spiritual when compared with herself. After digging a little deeper, I uncovered that while she meditated, chanted, and read spiritual books, he was dedicated to his global IT company and its 200 employees.

I asked her why she did not believe him to be a spiritual man when he was inspired by what he did, created jobs that supported 200 families, and routinely paid his taxes. She responded that she believed those to be material concerns and not what she regarded as spiritual. She did, however, appreciate how he supported her financially so she could dedicate her time completely to her version of inspired spiritual pursuits.

This woman, like many other individuals, had bought into the idea that spirituality should fit neatly into a particular box instead of seeing more fully how her husband, who was inspired by his work and who made a difference in the world, was just as spiritual as anyone else.

As we've seen, every human being on this planet has a unique set of values that spontaneously inspires them to pursue what is most important and deeply meaningful to them.

As I've already noted, I'm inspired by teaching, researching, writing and traveling the world. I wake up each morning inspired to teach, research, write, and travel. Others may feel uninspired by my particular spiritual path of teaching, researching human behavior, and sharing approaches that help maximize the potential of human beings. That inspires me, but it does not inspire everyone else. That's my spiritual path. But it is no more and no less spiritual than your particular spiritual path and what inspires you.

Throughout history, human beings have imaginatively created anthropomorphic deities and personified nature in order to understand their own lives and their relationship to the cosmos. But many of the religious models that have existed through time were just reflections of particular stages of awareness and brain development and our philic and phobic or loving interactions with whatever we perceive within or around us.

If you would love to awaken your own form of your spirituality, it is wiser to avoid becoming stagnant in the beliefs of the past and instead to keep evolving, growing, understanding, and living congruently with what you value most—your natural and spontaneous path of inspired or spiritual action. This will also be your greatest path of productivity.

And it's all spiritual. Some people may look at my life and perceive that it's hell because they are projecting their own highest value (perhaps time with family) onto me. Because of my travel and teaching schedule, I may spend less time with my family than they do. They can perceive this as wrong, concluding that I'm not spiritual.

But for me, living congruently with my highest values and helping human beings around the world transform their lives is expansive and heavenly.

I have yet to find a universally sustaining value system. Instead, each individual tends to think that their own system is right, often while giving their power over to a book, leader, or some outer authority. These are artificial approaches, trapping some of these individuals in non-resilient and intolerant states of mind and in-group and out-group biases. As I previously stated, it is all spiritual.

I think human beings demonstrate greater wisdom by digging deeper and have a broader and more relative overview, no longer narrowly perceiving events as solely or absolutely positive or negative or right and wrong,

If you choose not to look for or see the whole, you're probably being exclusive instead of inclusive. As such, you're less likely to maximize your potential or inspire and exemplify an authentic path of inspiration to other people and less likely to have maximum ripple effect and productivity.

The greatest teacher is example. One way to exemplify a spiritual path is to do what you truly love in a way that equally serves others. When you're doing something you're really inspired by, love, and can't wait to do, and that contributes to the lives of others, you're most likely to be fulfilled and grateful for your life. This is a worthy and inspired spiritual mission.

Pope John Paul II said that gratitude is heaven and ingratitude is hell. Think about your own life, and you will likely find that when you're grateful, your life is more expanded and heavenly. When you're ungrateful, you're likely to perceive that your life is hell. When you live in accordance with your true highest values, you expand and become grateful. When you don't, you shrink, and you feel unfulfilled.

Each event is neutral until somebody comes along with a subjective bias and makes a heaven or a hell out of it. This can be incredibly challenging for someone to hear when they have run a story for years about how their mother was never there for them or how their partner left them for someone else.

When I ask, "So what was the benefit?" it often throws them, because they have been so narrowly black-and-white in their thinking that it did not occur to them that there may be an equal number of upsides. If you are not conscious of both the upsides and downsides—the positives and negatives, losses and gains—in any trait or situation, you aren't fully conscious.

No matter what goes on in your life, if you see both sides of it, you can center yourself, come to a state of gratitude, be objective, resilient, and neutral, and come back into your flow. It has little or nothing to do with what's out there (over which you have little or no control), and everything to do with your perceptions, decisions, and actions (over which you do have control).

You have control over your sensory neurons, interneurons, and motor neurons. You can take whatever you perceive has happened and make a heaven or hell out of it when in fact it's neither. It's just what you choose to perceive.

If you see that there's nothing but a balanced state of complementary opposites, which make up a true state of inspired love, you are more effectively able to realize that it's all meaningful. Even ostensibly negative experiences are essential parts of your spiritual journey.

There's nothing but love; all else is a subjectively biased illusion. At first, many people struggle to understand this concept, because they perceive love as an infatuation and hate as its opposite. In truth, love is a synthesis and synchronicity of all possible complementary opposites at any scale of existence. When you realize that they come together as a pair, as great philosophers such as Heraclitus, Parmenides, and Hegel emphasized, you realize that there is nothing but love. That's why it's all inspirational. It is in this state of awareness that creativity and productivity abound.

It's about seeing both sides and bringing your percep-tions back into balance so you can see the whole. Running your personal dramatic narrative is not going to empower you. As another great Greek philosopher, Epictetus, said, first you blame others, then you blame yourself, and you finally come to realize that there's nothing and no one to blame and there's a hidden order in your life.

If you can take whatever happens in your life and find out how it's helping you fulfill what's most important and meaningful to you, you have no reason to say anything but thank you.

Everything you become infatuated with or resent rever-berates in your mind as noise and acts as an emotional dis-traction, which runs you, causes entropy in the body, and breaks you down. Most psychosomatic illnesses are auto-nomically initiated epigenetic expressions of imbalanced misperceptions and false, morally hypocritical labels that individuals impose on themselves, people, or events.

Once you ask equilibrating questions, become more fully conscious, and balance those events, you become lib-erated, and realize there was a hidden order in your appar-ent chaos. This can bring about a return to wellness.

Helping people find the hidden order in their chaos and the magnificence of their life is what inspires me. It's my path of meaning and inspiration. I love helping people unfold maximum productivity in their lives.

Every event acts as a feedback mechanism to guide you toward your most authentic self, your essential self, your soul (if you want to use the theological language for it), or your executive center (if you want to use the neurological term for it).

As far as I'm concerned, these terminologies all work. I can go in and out of philosophical, theological, scientific, psychological languages to discuss the same material, but ultimately, it's all inspirational, once we are fully conscious and perceive both sides simultaneously.

Giving yourself permission to see that it's all part of an inspirational path is a very liberating state, and knowing how to ask the questions to wake that awareness up is extremely powerful.

There's nothing in your life that you can't turn into an inspiring and gratitude generating experience if you know how to ask equilibrating questions. Productivity is not only about business and financial matters. Productivity is also about the other areas of life that matter.

The Healing Power of Unconditional Love

Most people believe that medical professionals and medication are what heal them. While they may be of great assistance at times, the greatest healing power lies within you. In fact, many medicines are more palliative than curative.

Let's take a step back and look at where illness, "disease," and symptomology originate—in what some have called the mind. When we are not well, our productivity diminishes.

As we've seen, when you meet someone you admire or become infatuated with and elevate them relative to you, you tend to minimize yourself in response. You exaggerate them and minimize you.

The opposite may also occur. You may minimize them relative to you and exaggerate yourself in response. You minimize them and exaggerate you.

Both are forms of judgment that result in your putting conditions, positive or negative valences, or emotional charges on both them and you. (*Valence*, or *valency*, is a term used to describe the subjective value of an event or individual in your life. An event or entity that you are conventionally attracted to has a positive valence, while one that repels you has a negative valence.)

You may not realize that when you exaggerate or minimize others relative to you, you may be either too humble or too proud to admit that what you see in them is also in you.

Whether you elevate or disparage someone else, you are necessarily perceiving incompletely. As we have already seen, you own all the traits: none are missing. So does the other individual, even though you may not see that fully.

But if you ignore certain aspects of yourself, seeing them in others but not in you, you have disowned parts, dismembered parts, and deflective awareness. Those deflected parts are voids that often leave you feeling empty. You are highly unlikely to judge another individual without feeling empty as a result.

Whenever you put someone on a pedestal or in a pit, and put yourself in a pit or on pedestal, you're being inauthentic. Neither expresses the authentic you. And you are not perceiving the authentic other.

You, like others, want to be loved for who you are, but if you're not being who you are, how do you imagine them being able to do that? Instead you may feel a partial sense of emptiness. That emptiness comes from the disowned parts of you that you're deflecting instead of owning.

How do these considerations relate to illness, dis-ease, wellness, healing, and ultimately productivity?

Your deflected, disowned parts, which leave you empty, also affect your nervous system and physiology.

The primitive, survival-oriented part of your inner subcortical brain, the amygdala, assigns valence to your perceptual experiences and to your perceptions of other individuals. It labels them as being either prey or predator, pleasurable or painful, positive or negative, attractive or repulsive, primarily as a result of previous subconsciously stored associations.

If you put someone on a pedestal, it represents them as *prey*: something positive that attracts you and makes you want to consume them with pleasure. You are most likely to want to be around people you put on pedestals.

When your brain assigns a positive valency, it activates your parasympathetic nervous system and causes a parasympathetic response, which is to rest and digest. As such, you will tend to seek out this individual and want to spend time with them. You'll tend to feel engaged and comfortable with them, and unlikely to feel defensive around them.

On the other hand, when you look down on someone and put them in a pit, they represent a *predator*: something that repels you and you want to avoid. When your brain assigns a negative valency, it activates the sympathetic nervous system, which governs fight-or-flight responses. Therefore you tend to avoid such individuals.

Over time, looking either up at someone or down on someone can result in dysregulation of your autonomic nervous system and physiology.

The autonomic nervous system is designed to help you survive through eating, avoiding being eaten, and maintaining autonomic and homeostatic balance. In fact, heart rate variability, which is a measure of resilience and adaptability, comes from a perfectly balanced autonomic function: when the sympathetic and parasympathetic are balanced. But whenever you have one side dominating the other, you create symptomatology and reduced resilience.

Symptomatology is mostly labeled as illness. However, this so-called illness might actually be a homeostatic feedback response involving your physiology to let you know that you have an imbalanced or valent perspective. In other words, you're likely judging someone instead of recognizing the balance of both sides and loving them.

Symptomatology offers feedback to let you know you're not balanced in your perception and not loving unconditionally. Nor are you being grateful for the order and balance that this individual represents and actually presents. You are not recognizing that they are helping you be more introspective and reflective and ultimately to own whatever you perceive in them and help you return to authenticity, or wholeness.

Again, it is your state of authenticity that maximizes your wellness and productivity.

Let's dig a little deeper.

As we've seen, when you put people on pedestals, you tend to inject some of their values into your life and want to change yourself relative to them, which is futile. If you try to inject their values, live in their values, and try to be like them, you will most likely end up breaking down.

If you are resentful toward someone and look down on them, you tend to project your own values onto them. You tend to want to change them relative to you and get them to live in your value system.

Whenever you try to get others to live in your value system or to get yourself to live in someone else's value system, you have futility and create symptomatology. The symptomatology is trying to let you know that you're likely judging instead of being grateful for the hidden order and balance that are present in the other individual and ultimately within yourself that you are being unconscious of, or overlooking.

When you understand that there's nothing to fix and nothing to change, in you or them you begin to acknowledge a loving hidden order. You don't experience subordination or superordination, only ordination. Your physiology won't need to create autonomic and epigenetic symptoms to wake you up, resulting in wholeness or wellness.

Wellness is mostly a confirmation that you are perceiving what actually is, while illness is mostly feedback to let you know you're not fully perceiving the whole picture.

I strongly believe that gratitude and love are still the greatest healers. But people don't pay attention to the subtle feedback attempting to wake them up to this truth. Instead, they are wedded to a palliative healthcare system that is based on the amygdala's response of avoiding pain and seeking pleasure. This is sometimes called the magic bullet, or opium of the masses.

The second people have a symptom, they assume that it relates to illness instead of considering that it just might be feedback to help guide them back to balance, authenticity, gratitude, love, and wellness. Physiologist Walter Cannon once called it "the wisdom of the body."

If you take a pill for every ill, and you cover it up with palliative care, you'll likely end up not embracing the lesson and wisdom that your body is trying to give you. (Of course, palliative care has a place in emergency or terminal settings.)

Taking a pill to suppress or counterbalance your symptoms instead of listening to your body's feedback and learning from it is not necessarily the wisest way to approach healing and wellness. It's wiser to learn to interpret what your physiology is trying to tell you.

Your body is doing everything it can to teach you how to love and be authentic and grateful for the hidden order that life offers. The hidden order is actually there, even though you may be unconscious of part of your reality and perceive chaos. The order is only hidden because you're not aware of it. The order in your life is there; you're just not perceiving it.

When you judge, you have emptiness and disowned parts. When you love, you have fulfillment and integration. When you have unconditional love, there are no disowned parts. When you're neither too humble nor too proud to admit what you see in others is also inside you, you own it all. There's nothing missing in you. When you do, you have fulfillment. It is in this state that maximum productivity and inspiration are born.

Appendix

Enhance Your Reading Powers

To sum up: the key to true productivity is to acknowledge and design your life according to your own highest values, act and serve in accordance with them, delegate tasks of lower priority to others and become fully conscious of the ever present hidden order. You can overcome inner obstacles by acknowledging that whatever you see in another individual also exists in yourself and understanding that each positive is balanced by a corresponding negative, and vice versa. Once you realize this fact, you open up the gateways of greater productivity and energy.

I would like to end this book with a more specific way of doubling your productivity: enhanced reading. This chapter is designed to open you up to the potential of this amazing boost to your learning capacities.

Reading more rapidly and organizing your learning will help you awaken your genius, creativity and productivity.

I would love you to imagine that as you learn, you're going to expand your horizons. As Emerson shared in his essay "Circles," your most authentic self, or what theologians have called your soul, continually calls you to ever greater expanses.

Imagine that you're starting from a small sphere of awareness and expanding it toward the infinite. Every time you read, you bring out of yourself truths that you inherently and innately sense and know. In fact, reading draws out of you what you already know. You may have noticed that when you have read certain observations, you somehow resonated with them and knew them to be true.

Reading allows you to explore the universe through others' eyes. Devouring a high-quality book can save you time, because it enables you to take advantage of another's entire lifetime of understanding in a few hours. It also allows you to avoid reinventing wheels. If you can stand on the shoulders of giants through reading, you can find out what a whole lineage of people have explored. You can live more wisely and productively by foresight instead of hindsight or trial and error. Then you can pick up where they left off and become a pioneer. You can also learn to transcend the primordial boundary between yourself and others.

We've already seen that we're most disciplined, reliable, and focused in respect to what's highest on our list of values. Consequently, you will have the most discipline, reliability, and focus when what you're reading is aligned to your highest values. You will organize the knowledge and identify with it, and it will stay with you, because it will *be* you. If you go down to the lower values, you will encounter procrastination, hesitation, and frustration. You will tend to bring disorder and disorganization, and you will disown this material. You don't identify with it.

In short, as you're attempting to read, it's wise to ask, "How will reading this specific book, chapter, article, topic, or material help me fulfill my highest value?" This will help you more masterfully absorb, retain, and apply the information you are now more inspired to devour.

Here's one way to begin. Write down in one sentence exactly how you would love to read. The French philosopher René Descartes wrote down a statement saying, "My dream is to be a man of letters. I want to have an encyclopedic mind." He attained this end. You might want to say to yourself (stating your intention as an affirmation of what you already possess), "I have an encyclopedic mind. Whatever I read, I retain. I'm a genius, with an amazing capacity to absorb, store, and disseminate information."

The next step is to organize your time. Plan your reading. Which authors and which books or articles would you love to read? Where, when, and how do you love to read? Define your highest value–based purpose for reading. Once you put the infrastructure in place, the functions will follow: function follows structure.

Set a time each day when you know you can most consistently read and you can make a habit of it. If you make a habit of it, it becomes your new norm. Also, set a deadline on your reading—for a certain number of books by a certain date—and put yourself under your own challenging, but still realistic, commitment.

Some of my students have created what they call "mindfulness evenings." They write book summaries and get together to share them. Every week or month, they have a group of fifteen or twenty people, sometimes more, sometimes less, who have committed to getting together. Each participant is accountable for bringing books and summarizing them for the others. As a result, they're challenged to read, they have deadlines, and they get more out of themselves. They are more productive. When you hear somebody speak, you remember at least some of what they're saying; similarly with material you discuss or share. Moreover, if you are accountable to present material, you make sure you're ready. So evenings of mindfulness and sharing book clubs can be very valuable. Another advantage to this approach: if you know you're going to read books as a group, you can buy them at a discount. (Of course, many books are also available on Google, Bing, Amazon, and the Internet.)

Make sure to read quality books. Write down how many books you read per month at your current pace. Write down that number. Then multiply that by 12, and then multiply that number times the number of years you expect to live. If you read 3 books a month, that's 36 books a year. If you expect to live another 30 years, that amounts to 960 books that you will read over the rest of your life.

In any event, that number is finite. Therefore don't you think it would be wise, instead of reading at random, to plan what you're going to read? Remember, any area of your life you don't empower, somebody else will overpower. If you do not full your day with high-priority reading it will fill with low-priority reading.

Organize Your Reading

I've found it very productive to plan my reading. Of course, that doesn't mean you can't do some spontaneous reading in between, but I do believe it's wise to plan your readings. When I started reading in a given discipline, I would look in the bibliography and find the origins of that discipline. For example, if you want to explore evolutionary biology, you might start with Charles Darwin's earthshaking classic *The Origin of Species.* If you're interested in magnetism, you might start with William Gilbert's *De magnete* ("On the Magnet").

After reading the originators, I would look at the development and evolution of the discipline. Disciplines generally evolve by a dialectic oscillation: people would advance a given idea, and others would dispute it. Nevertheless, the later commentators were very seldom as inspiring as the originator. Rarely do people who comment on Aristotle really get the depth of what Aristotle was about.

I think that everybody could benefit by reading the two volumes of the *Syntopicon: An Index to the Great Ideas* in the Encylopaedia Brittanica's Great Books of the Western World series. In this work, the editors catalogued what they deemed to be the fundamental ideas contained in the great books of Western civilization, from Homer to Freud.

They summarize the greatest ideas from the greatest minds over the last three millennia. They give you an overview of the greatest thinking, enabling you to absorb it most efficiently. I find that reading masterpieces written by great minds generate innovative ideas within and are therefore highly productive uses of time.

You cannot put your hand into a pot of glue without having some of the glue sticking. In the same way, you cannot put your mind into the great works of the immortal masters without having some of their ideas stick. I don't keep up with fad books today, because I don't consistently find as much truly insightful and meaningful content there. One immortal classic is worth 1,000 mortal fads. One quality, classic book by Emerson or William James can beat most of the self-help books on the market.

Is there any part of you that desires to master your life and leave a lasting or an immortal effect on the world—an achievement that will last beyond your life? If so, instead of denying that, admit it: "I want to be a master. I want to leave an immortal effect on the planet." If you want to do it, don't lie to yourself; admit it and increase the odds that it will happen. Emerson says that nothing is any value in books except the transcendent and extraordinary. When you fill your mind with inspired ideas, your mind absorbs the information and creates new concepts. It is from this expanded state that maximum creativity and productivity emerge.

Determine what you want to read and how much you want to read. Decide the most useful and important reading that will enable you to fulfill what you truly dream about and how you want to be remembered in this planet. Just stopping to ask that question may launch you into new priorities and new levels of productivity.

When you read, it is wise to also have time for reflection.

Your objective is to *read, retain,* and *reflect.* Also realize that if you absorb someone's idea on a given topic, it can sway you in a direction with their subjective bias, which may not be to your greatest advantage. So reading multiple texts and authors on both sides of the dialectic can give you a greater and more holistic picture. This is one of the reasons for and advantages of becoming a polymath.

Let me give you an example. When I was about eighteen, the first area I wanted to study was nutrition. I started reading books on the subject, and I got confused. It seemed that there were contradictory opinions about practically every detail. Then I started to organize the information. I created a chart so I could compile everything that I read on vitamins and nutrients and other nutritional subjects. After a while, I started seeing a pattern. I saw that each author had their own bias and pet products, and each was counterbalanced by others.

After reading a couple of hundred books on nutrition, I put these ideas into context and saw a cohesive whole. Reading one source can bias you, but reading enough sources can put them into context. My objective was to avoid being swayed by single opinions while extracting the more universal principles and reflecting on these. If you read one book, it can become your authority, but if you read many, *you* eventually become your authority.

Emotions in Reading

If you are like most individuals, you've probably noticed moments in your day when you feel elevated and moments where you feel a bit down; this occurs in an oscillating pattern. The mind goes through cycles: when you're elated, time speeds up; when you're depressed, it slows down. Your emotions, like gravity, perceptually or actually distort the fabric of space-time.

You're going to have emotions throughout the day. If you're in the center, between the extremes, you feel grateful, you feel loved, you're inspired and enthusiastic. And you are more certain and present. This is the most powerful and productive state to read in. That's why reading material linked to your highest values enables you to be most predictably poised and centered when you read. If not, you're going to go up and down, and experience highs and lows.

Your brain has a feedback system to help you read in this centered state. You have a right brain for a fast pace and a left brain for a slow pace. The left brain breaks objects and events down into parts. You read slowly and get only letters and words. With the right brain, you tend to read holistically, so you can read fast and get a whole picture.

Let's look at what happens in the mind here. Your left hemisphere involves vocal reading. Most people who read that way believe that one slow reading is greater than ten fast readings. They read linearly and have sequential comprehension. They read letters, syllables, words, and phrases. They remember and recall by means of sound. They judge their reading; they remain more intellectual and less intuitive; they actively search and read for specific details; they verbalize and vocalize what they read; and they read about 250 words a minute. They're more receptive to adjectives and adverbs, and they let the words do the painting. Left-brain reading is slow.

The right-brain reader believes that a few fast readings are greater than one slow reading, so they can read a few times faster. They read nonlinearly and have holistic comprehension. They read sentences, paragraphs, and pages in a single picture. Because they're visual, they review and reexperience instead of recalling. They are less likely to judge what they read. They let their intuition allow them to know that they've gotten it holistically. They passively, receptively allow for highlights, concepts, and general principles. They visualize what they read. They're actively receptive to nouns and verbs instead of adjectives and adverbs, and they let the pictures do the talking.

To master reading, you have the opportunity to use both approaches. It's not necessarily better to read fast. Reading slowly has a place; in fact, you want to allow yourself to do both. Most people have no problem reading slowly, they just haven't mastered fast reading, but there's a time for each one.

Tips for Optimal Reading

As with any activity, there are optimal conditions for reading. Let me go through some of the most basic and important ones.

Fresh air. When you're reading, make sure you have fresh air, because oxygen is a stimulant. Carbon dioxide, CO_2, is a sedative. Rising CO_2 concentrations will put you to sleep. The more oxygen you have, the more awake you're going to be.

Water. I primarily drink water, because it's the universal solvent: it keeps the cells in the brain functioning most effectively. On the other hand, drinks with sugar cloud the brain. Stimulants and sugars also tend to make you more emotionally volatile, decreasing your capacity to learn.

Use the dictionary. Have a dictionary next to you. Dictionaries enable you to expand your vocabulary and understanding. Look up any word that you don't understand. Your reading, along with your vocabulary, affects your opportunities. If you go to the house of an impoverished family, you may not find any books at all; the higher you go on the socioeconomic ladder, the more books you are likely to find in the house, and the more productivity you will generally find at the office.

Diffuse light. Make sure you have diffuse light, because you can't see very clearly if you've got shadows and glares. Don't read under direct sunlight. Don't read lying down, looking at a book when you're sunbathing and the sun's glaring. You'll probably fall asleep in minutes.

Moderate temperature. Have the temperature around 68 to 72 degrees Fahrenheit. If it's just a little on the cool side, it's preferable; if it's warm, it'll tend to put you to sleep.

Loose clothing and posture. I recommend loose clothing, such as yoga clothes. I used to wear nothing more than yoga pants. Sit upright and have the book angled, so you don't create problems with your neck. If your cerebrospinal fluid is able to move, you will tend to stay awake, whereas slouching can block the flow of your cerebrospinal fluid, and you tend to slow down or go to sleep.

Eye angle. Your eyes can go down about twenty or twenty-five degrees, because if your head is down all day long, you're going to tighten up and create an osteophytic growth in the back of your skull. I had to learn that the hard way.

Preview and review. Once you have the right environment, it is wise to preview and review the book. Pull it out, look at the front and back cover, look at the title, look at the subtitle, and look at the authors. The title and the subtitle give you an idea of what the book is about. Information about the authors gives you an idea of their credibility. Are they scientists? Are they novelists? Their biographies will enable you to see the book's background and substance.

Then look at the copyright page, which will tell you the date of the book's original publication. If you're reading a book on computers and it's from 1940, you're probably not going to get information that's accurate today.

Read the preface, which can give you an idea of whether or not the book is worth your time. Effective and productive reading is not just a matter of speed: it's also deciding what you want to read and what is priority.

Look at the bibliography, the glossary, and the index. Look at the pictures, because sometimes a picture with a caption will summarize a whole chapter, or, in a magazine, the whole article. Once you know that information, you may not desire to read the whole text.

Read the summaries, headings, and subheadings; some authors italicize or boldface the most important points. Sometimes the first sentence or paragraph of the chapter summarizes the whole, enabling you to determine whether or not it's worth your time.

Some authors, especially in the academic world, write summaries or article abstracts. If you read them, you get the essence of the article. Part of reading is learning how to be efficient in reading, and not just reading unnecessarily.

Love the author. Occasionally, you'll read about a subject toward which you have a bias in one direction or another. You may feel infatuated with or resentful toward the author. As a result, you can be gullible or skeptical, and you're probably going to get a biased interpretation. Make sure you have a balanced orientation with respect to the author, whether you agree with them or not. If you don't, consider using the Demartini Method to balance your perceptual equation.

Be present. If you're present, you'll retain the information more. So let's look at how you read. In English, you begin at the upper left, go across the lines, and down to the lower right. Therefore the left and top parts of the page represent the past remembered on the page; the right and lower parts represent the future imagined. The "present" or "now" represents wherever and whenever you're the focal point of your vision is seemingly fixed.

Use the focal point. As your mind is going across the page, your focus is going across it as well. If you're inspired by your reading and it's linked to your highest value–based purpose, your focal point—what you see—expands. You're alert, and you want to grasp the material. As your focal point expands, you're going to see more of your picture. If the content is not inspiring to you, your focal point shrinks, and you're going to see less of your picture.

If as you read, you focus on the top of the lowercase letters and the middle of the uppercase letters, you will maximize the area encompassed by the focal point. In the average reader, if their eyes are two feet away from the book, their fovea (an area in the eye of maximum visual acuity and color discrimination) will see 3±2 letters as a focal point.

When your eye is centered and steady, it sees from a centered and poised state of love and widens its central vision, thereby including more of the peripheral vision. When your eye is not centered or steadied but is wandering, it sees in the past or future and narrows its central vision, missing much of its peripheral vision.

Your eyes make small movements, even around a dot, to maintain contrast and prevent fading. They strive to centralize their focal point at whatever level of the reading dynamic they view, whether it be a whole page, paragraph, sentence, phrase, word, syllable, or letter.

Use a visual guide. Use either a finger, pencil, or marker while you read. Otherwise your eyes are going to wander around in a jerky fashion rather than moving smoothly along the page. If you use a visual guide, your eyes can stay steadily on track. This will enlarge the central focal point and reduce distractions and mental wandering, as well as backward skipping or forward skipping.

Read in three-hour segments. I've gotten into a second wind when I did three-hour segments of reading: a forty-five-minute session; a break; forty-five minutes; break; forty-five minutes; break. During breaks:

- Review in your head what you've just read. Stop, close your eyes, and reflect. What did I just read? How does that help me fulfill my mission? How does it help me fulfill my highest value? How's that going to help me fulfill my life? Take a few seconds to think about those questions. Whenever you link what you are reading to your highest values, you will increase your absorption, assimilation, retention, and utilization or application.

- Drink some water.

- Stand up and stretch backward and forward as you inhale and exhale deeply. Inhale deeply as you extend back, and then exhale as you flex forward. Inhale through the nose; get the oxygen. Make sure your neck and shoulders go out and back in order to counterbalance your previous posture. Do this about five times.

- Exercise and stretch your eye muscles by looking

Up	Right down
Down	Left down
Right	Far
Left	Close
Right up	Centrally
Left up	Peripherally

This exercise is to relax the eye muscles and make sure they are used in all their variations. Otherwise, with one constant movement going back and forth, they'll get muscle-bound, which increases the probability of eye problems. Many eye problems occur simply because the muscles are not being used properly. Astigmatism, nearsightedness, and farsightedness have a bit to do with the functioning of the eye muscles.

- Briskly rub your palms until they are warmed up. Then, keeping your eyes open, cover them thoroughly with your palms. This calms the eyes after the previous exercise has stretched them.

Double Your Reading

Just with what we've done here, would you agree that you could double your reading? If you double the number of words you read, you double the number of texts you read in your life, and you have halved the time it takes to read. As you grow more comfortable with this process, you can triple or quadruple your reading speed by linking your reading content to your purpose and using the other techniques I've already discussed.

One point to note: when most people read, without knowing it, they are using their occipital visual cortex. Researchers have found that if you look and think about a given area of the body, you will increase the blood flow to that area. If you look at or think about your finger, you will get an increased blood supply to the finger. In the same, if you think about a region of your brain, you increase the amount of blood supply and oxygen it receives. If you read from your eyes and think about your eyes, you will get red eyes. But if you read from the back of your brain, you will have the highest retention. Don't read from your eyes; read from the back of the head. This way, you'll have the greatest ability to retain information, associate it with other material, and avoid making your eyes red. You'll be able to read for a longer period of time.

Create a Master Mind group. Here's another useful and fun technique. As I read some of the most amazing originators of material, I felt that they had become my friends, so I started creating a Master Mind group that I would read with. I plugged in these great minds like a computer cable, so I had all their knowledge when I was reading. As a result, there was little or nothing new when I read; it was all just review.

In short, read while imagining yourself using another genius's brain. It's a mind game, but it's a powerful one. My first one was Albert Einstein. He was my favorite. I read everything that was written by Albert Einstein that was available. I wanted to know his work because he was considered one of the great geniuses. I imagined Albert with me.

In this way, you accumulate leaders in the field you're studying. Believe it or not, if you're reading a book on money and you plug in Warren Buffett, Bill Gates, or Peter Lynch, I guarantee that you're going to get a different perspective. Your perspective on them and whatever you know about them is now being filtered into what you're studying, and your confidence goes up.

Read from different parts of your body. Imagine you're reading from the back of the head first, then go over to the shoulder, and imagine that your consciousness is coming from your shoulder through your body. The different body parts will get different information out of the page.

Reading and Self-Enhancement

One primary means to gain more skills and knowledge and to enhance your creativity and productivity is through reading. The word *read* comes from the Old English *raedan*, which means *to advise oneself.*

Reading allows you to explore the universe.

Reading keeps you from reinventing wheels.

Reading allows you to surpass the primordial boundary between yourself and others.

Reading allows the seer, the seeing, and the seen to be the same.

Reading allows you to honor the logos, or the reason and intelligent order of the universe, by exploring the various ologies.

Reading allows you to study the many disciplines of life, which will enable you to become more well-rounded and inwardly "disciplined"—a disciple of the logos, or the hidden order of the universe.

It's possible to enhance your reading skills to the point where you can read hundreds of pages in an hour, but this is a more specialized study. Even the simple techniques given here can help you read far more rapidly and with greater retention. This expanded opportunity to double your learning will give you a competitive advantage and enable you to be more productive in less time.

My fifty years of multidisciplinary research across many fields of inquiry has allowed me to become polymathic, which has provided me with many inspiring opportunities that I am certain would not have arisen had I limited my knowledge and not linked it to my chief aim. You too can receive many inspiring rewards by expanding your knowledge, linking it to what you value most, and pursuing what is deeply meaningful to you in a way that greatly serves others.

Thank you for reading *The Productivity Factor*. May you now give yourself permission to do something inspiring and extraordinary on planet earth and accomplish at least twice as much in half the time.

About the Author

Dr. John Demartini is a human behavioral specialist and founder of the Demartini Institute, a private research and education institute dedicated to activating leadership and human potential. He's an international best-selling author and business consultant, working with CEOs of Fortune 500 companies, celebrities, and sports personalities. Globally, he's worked with individuals and groups across many markets, including entrepreneurs, financiers, psychologists, teachers, and young adults, assisting and guiding them to greater levels of achievement, fulfillment, and empowerment in many areas of their lives.

For more information about Dr. John Demartini, his live events, and products and services, contact the Demartini Institute on info@drdemartini.com. To view his website, visit www.drdemartini.com.

9 781722 506292